Chaucer: The Canterbury Tales

ANALYSING TEXTS

General Editor: Nicholas Marsh

Chaucer: The Canterbury Tales *Gail Ashton*

Shakespeare: The Tragedies *Nicholas Marsh*

Virginia Woolf: The Novels *Nicholas Marsh*

Jane Austen: The Novels *Nicholas Marsh*

Thomas Hardy: The Novels *Norman Page*

Further titles are in preparation

Analysing Texts
Series Standing Order ISBN 0–333–73260–X
(*outside North America only*)

You can receive future titles in this series as they are published by placing a standing order. Please contact your bookseller or, in case of difficulty, write to us at the address below with your name and address, the title of the series and the ISBN quoted above.

Customer Services Department, Macmillan Distribution Ltd
Houndmills, Basingstoke, Hampshire RG21 6XS, England

Chaucer: The Canterbury Tales

GAIL ASHTON

First published 1998 by
MACMILLAN PRESS LTD
Houndmills, Basingstoke, Hampshire RG21 6XS
and London
Companies and representatives throughout the world

ISBN 0–333–73932–9 hardback
ISBN 0–333–69406–6 paperback

A catalogue record for this book is available from the British Library.

This book is printed on paper suitable for recycling and made from fully managed and sustained forest sources.

10 9 8 7 6 5 4 3 2 1
07 06 05 04 03 02 01 00 99 98

Printed and bound in Great Britain by
Butler & Tanner Ltd, Frome and London

Published in the United States of America 1998 by
ST. MARTIN'S PRESS, INC.,
Scholarly and Reference Division,
175 Fifth Avenue, New York, N.Y. 10010

ISBN 0–312–21376–X cloth
ISBN 0–312–21377–8 paperback

Contents

General Editor's Preface

This series is dedicated to one clear belief: that we can all enjoy, understand and analyse literature for ourselves, provided we know how to do it. How can we build on close understanding of a short passage, and develop our insight into the whole work? What features do we expect to find in a text? Why do we study style in so much detail? In demystifying the study of literature, these are only some of the questions the *Analysing Texts* series addresses and answers.

The books in this series will not do all the work for you, but will provide you with the tools, and show you how to use them. Here, you will find samples of close, detailed analysis, with an explanation of the analytical techniques utilised. At the end of each chapter there are useful suggestions for further work you can do to practise, develop and hone the skills demonstrated and build confidence in you own analytical ability.

An author's individuality shows in the way they write: every work they produce bears the hallmark of that writer's personal 'style'. In the main part of each book we concentrate, therefore, on analysing the particular flavour and concerns of one author's work, and explain the features of their writing in connection with major themes. In Part 2 there are chapters about the author's life and work, assessing their contribution to developments in literature; and a sample of critics' views are summarised and discussed in comparison with each other. Some suggestions for further reading provide a bridge towards further critical research.

Analysing Texts is designed to stimulate and encourage your critical and analytic faculty, to develop your personal insight into the author's work and individual style, and to provide you with the skills and techniques to enjoy at first hand the excitement of discovering the richness of the text.

NICHOLAS MARSH

Acknowledgements

The author and publishers wish to thank the following for permission to use copyright material:

Houghton Mifflin Company for extracts from Larry D. Benson, General Editor, *The Riverside Chaucer*, Third edition. Copyright © 1987 by Houghton Mifflin Company.

Every effort has been made to trace the copyright holders but if any have been inadvertently overlooked the publishers will be pleased to make the necessary arrangement at the first opportunity.

PART 1

PRACTICAL EXAMPLES OF ANALYSIS

1

An Introduction to Chaucer

Geoffrey Chaucer wrote *The Canterbury Tales* almost 600 years ago, in the late Middle Ages, a historical distance that at first sight might appear problematic. This lengthy poem was produced at a time when the English language was still in its infancy and the language is not always immediately recognisable to us today. In the same way, late medieval culture was very different from that of the present day.

Yet these are only *apparent* difficulties. The differences are soon identified and soon understood. Rather than being a stumbling block to study, they instead enrich and enhance our appreciation. My hope is that in reading this book you too will come to an enthusiastic understanding of why Chaucer might merit the adjective 'great'.

It is useful to note that there are several ways of reading the *Tales*, none of which provides a conclusive answer on its own. The first thing to mention is the need to approach Chaucer and his work with an open mind. The poems in *The Canterbury Tales* might simply be enjoyed at the level upon which they first stand, as a series of varied stories – some serious, some highly entertaining, some elegant in style, some bawdy and coarse. Each poem can be read, explored and admired as a stand-alone text, a tale in its own right bearing little relation to its companions elsewhere in the *Tales*.

Equally, the stories which are told as part of a fictional drama, a storytelling contest organised for a band of pilgrims on their way to Canterbury, might be seen as part of a dramatic framework that, however inconsistently, holds the *Tales* together. This raises several questions. What is the relationship between the individual tales? Are some told as contrasts to others, or in a deliberate attempt to undercut ideas presented in other stories? Are some tales told in revenge, as part of a notion of 'quiting', or as part of a quarrel or dialogue between individual speakers? Is there any relationship between tale and teller, between fictional narrator and fiction, or even between speaker(s) and Chaucer himself? What is the role of the narrator in this make-believe contest (the 'I' of the *Tales*), or of Harry Bailly, the Host?

As readers we are drawn into this complex dramatic structure, and puzzled when the framework seems to disintegrate or even disappear altogether. At the same time it is not always clear who is telling these stories, or whose 'voice' or viewpoint is to be believed. Similarly, we need to ask ourselves why so many themes and ideas occur and reoccur in this long poem, or why Chaucer heaps multiplication upon multiplication with fascinating and dazzling frequency, each small irony casting new light upon the one before, so that in the end all definitive answers are resisted.

Only one thing is certain in *The Canterbury Tales*, and that is that Chaucer is a slippery and ambiguous writer. The joy (and the pain!) lies in the fact that he lends himself so beautifully to exploration and interpretation, to every theoretical and critical model available, and, ultimately, to your own personal viewpoint.

The aim of this study is to help you formulate that informed, exploratory and uniquely personal view. Throughout, the book raises more questions than it answers, asking you to address a variety of issues and complexities. Though it focuses upon a small selection of work from *The Canterbury Tales*, it is designed to help you develop your own critical faculties and form your own judgements. Part 1 is devoted to close reading and detailed analysis of short pieces of text, always followed by conclusions summarising the techniques used to explore them. In addition there is a reading section intended to extend your knowledge, and stimulate further ideas. Part 2 discusses Chaucer's life and works, and provides a sample from a range of critical views adopted by four critics, chosen for their relevance to the same poems we focus on in Part 1 as well as for their interesting opinions.

When you begin to read Chaucer, probably your first need is to become familiar with the language he uses. This will happen much more quickly than you might expect, and the following few hints can speed up the process even more.

The main thing to remember is that at the time that Chaucer was writing English was not standard, whether spoken or written, but composed of a series of regional dialects with much variation. Latin remained the official language for important documents or in the Church, while the main tongue, especially in court circles, was French. English began to be used more frequently in Chaucer's era but was still varied. The style used by the poet tends to be based upon the London or Kentish region, itself subject to influence from the east and central midlands. For written documents there was no consistent system of spelling, so there are frequent switches between forms. For example, the letter 'y' might denote our modern 'g' as in 'yeven' (given), or might represent the vowel 'i' so that there exists both 'lif' and 'lyf' (life). Similarly, the sound 'ou' might be represented as 'you' or 'yow'.

Even so, there is no need to 'learn' Middle English like a foreign language. The easiest way to understand it is by common sense and informed guesswork for most words sound like our own. One thing to remember is that many words are accented in the French manner with the stress on later syllables rather than the first as in English. There was a tendency to pronounce words in the French way too, hence the prevalence of words deriving from that language, like 'daunce' (dance), 'servyse' (service), 'flour' (flower), 'nacioun' (nation), 'penaunce' (penance), or 'remembraunce' (remembrance). Sometimes there is a stress on the final 'e' as in French songs, in words like 'wrecche' or 'fresshe', while there is also a Germanic or Scottish-sounding influence with harsh sounding 'ch' or 'gh' in 'doghtren' (daughter). The best way to understand what it all might have sounded like is to listen to one of the many professional tapes currently available. If you are embarrassed to read Chaucer aloud, then just modernise it; nine times out of ten the meaning will remain consistent with modern usage, as in words like 'werkyng' (working), 'philosofre' (philosopher), 'fals' (false), 'feendly' (fiendly), or 'shette the dore' (shut the door).

Most editions supply a glossary with the text as well as footnotes to translate the more difficult aspects. Though most words mean exactly what they sound like in modern-day English, you will soon learn the exceptions. Some, like 'gentillesse', have no exact equivalent, our 'gentility' lacking the strength of the original. Others, such as 'daungerous', have shifted meaning so that the word meant 'standoffish' or 'aloof' rather than 'dangerous'. Some words are specific to the medieval context though they occasionally still occur in certain dialect forms – words like 'wight' for 'person', 'likerous' for 'lecherous', or 'reweth' for 'regret'. Others have several meanings, so that 'corage' may mean, as expected, 'courage', but in other contexts imply 'sexual desire' or 'heart'. Certain tag or filler words are easily learnt – 'whilom' for 'once' or 'once upon a time', 'eek' for 'also', 'sikerly' for 'truly'. Soon recognised too are peculiarities of verb form ('maken', 'maden', 'to dyen' simply meaning 'make', 'made', 'to die'), and an odd syntax that only requires rearranging as in 'Me thynketh it' (it seems to me), 'it reweth me' (I regret it), or 'That knoweth I wel' (I know that well).

Finally, negatives merit a special mention. Usually signified by 'ne', they are often strengthened by the inclusion of others like 'nat' or 'noughte'/'noghte' in the same sentence or phrase. There may even be a series of words, all in negative forms, as in this example:

> 'He nevere yet no vileynye ne seyde
> ...unto no maner wight'.
> (He never spoke ill of anybody)

The effect is still negative.

2

Style and Narrative Skills

I: CHARACTERISATION AND PLOT – THE *MILLER'S TALE* AND THE WIFE OF BATH'S PORTRAIT

Chaucer's *The Canterbury Tales* is a melting pot of themes and ideas expressed in a rich mix of styles and techniques, mingling the comic and the serious, entertainment and instruction. Perhaps because many of the individual poems within the *Tales* can be categorised by genre or type of story (rather like the way a fairy story differs from a thriller), many examination questions focus upon Chaucer's style as if this is potentially a problem or a distinct entity unrelated to other ideas. Yet, as you read these poems, it soon becomes clear that style, characterisation, and narration form part of an overall impression *alongside* themes and purpose.

Is there then a difficulty concerning Chaucer's style? A reading of any extract chosen at random will soon show that Chaucer's work hinges upon characters and characterisation, and to some extent upon the personality of each tale's teller. Take the following extract from the *Miller's Tale*. As you first read this passage, you might like to consider a few questions.

What impression do you get of Absolon from a first reading? How is this portrait drawn? What details are we given?

> Now was ther of that chirche a parissh clerk,
> The which that was ycleped Absolon.
> Crul was his heer, and as the gold it shoon,

And strouted as a fanne large and brode;
Ful streight and evene lay his joly shode.
His rode was reed, his eyen greye as goos.
With Poules wyndow corven on his shoos,
In hoses rede he wente fetisly.
Yclad he was ful smal and proprely
Al in a kirtel of a lyght waget;
Ful faire and thikke been the poyntes set.
And therupon he hadde a gay surplys
As whit as is the blosme upon the rys.
A myrie child he was, so God me save.
Wel koude he laten blood, and clippe and / shave,
And maken a chartre of lond or acquitaunce.
In twenty manere koude he trippe and daunce
After the scole of Oxenforde tho,
And with his legges casten to and fro,
And pleyen songes on a smal rubible;
Therto he song som tyme a loud quynyble;
And as wel koude he pleye on a giterne.
In al the toun nas brewhous ne taverne
That he ne visited with his solas,
Ther any gaylard tappestere was.
But sooth to seyn, he was somdeel squaymous
Of fartyng, and of speche daungerous.

(1(A), ll.3312–38)

Absolon, it is said, has curled golden hair arranged in an elaborate hairstyle, 'strouted as a fanne large and brode' with a pretty parting or 'joly shode'. He has a pleasantly 'reed' complexion and grey eyes. He wears 'smal' or close-fitting clothes, a red hose, a light blue tunic carefully laced. He also has a 'gay' surplice, white as blossom, and shoes 'With Poules wyndow' carved on the leather as decoration. These details of physical appearance and clothing suggest, at first glance, an attractive elegance further enhanced by what the text tells of his dancing, singing and musical accomplishments, all indicating that he is a lively entertaining fellow, fond of a good time and with an eye for a 'gaylard tappestere', for the ladies.

A closer or subsequent reading of this passage might, however, undercut or qualify this impression in some way. Taken separately, his accomplishments appear delightful. He can dance, play the fiddle and the cithern or 'giterne', sing in 'a loud quynyble' and is full of 'solas' or entertainment. But put together in this way, these same details offer a more subtle or ironic portrait.

Absolon's singing and dancing cast him in the mould of a would-be courtly lover. Though he visits ale-houses to admire the women there are no details of his success with them. His social world is a relatively lowly one. He is a jack-of-all-trades, a hairdresser, able to let blood (a minor medical accomplishment), a humble clerk. His entertainment is found in taverns and ale-houses, yet he himself is dressed in elegant finery. A return to the details of Absolon's hair and clothing now suggest a vain, fastidious fellow, over-dressed for the occasion, a dedicated follower of fashion with his fine shoes and Oxford style of dancing. He is a figure of fun. His huge hairdo adds to the hint of effeminacy in his portrait, an impression reinforced by the narrator's almost sly aside in the closing lines of the passage. (It might help here to remember who the narrator is and what sort of person it is suggested he might be.)

Earlier, the effect of Absolon's clever dancing has been undercut with a single word 'tho' making clear this speaker's amusement:

> 'In twenty manere koude he trippe and daunce
> After the scole of Oxenforde tho.'

Later he adds 'But sooth to seyn', his aside informing us that Absolon is

> 'somdeel squaymous
> Of fartyng.'

The use of this down-to-earth word is deliberately shocking and out of place, and is highlighted by the line break. It indicates that Absolon is over-fastidious, not entirely masculine, an impression reinforced by the additional comment that, as his speech is 'daungerous', he is likely to be easily offended by the use of such colloquial language as well as the very idea of farting itself.

What a closer reading of this passage has suggested is that

Chaucer uses the technique of describing physical appearance, clothing, habits and pastimes, even occupation, to make his characters appear 'real'. It also suggests, however, that such surface details are not always to be taken at face value. Taken as a whole, rather than individually, a different picture might emerge, one which qualifies our original impression. Individual words or phrases can also undercut this initial portrait. Chaucer's tone is thus often ironic and his characterisation humorous or satirical.

To test this theory, glance at a range of other characterisations. Look at the way Alison or John are described in the same poem, or take at random any portrait from the *General Prologue*. What about the Miller himself, the teller of this tale, or the Wife of Bath, the subject of our next extract?

A good WIF was ther Of biside BATHE,
But she was somdeel deef, and that was scathe.
Of clooth-makyng she hadde swich an haunt
She passed hem of Ypres and of Gaunt.
In al the parisshe wif ne was ther noon
That to the offrynge bifore hire sholde goon;
And if ther dide, certeyn so wrooth was she
That she was out of alle charitee.
Hir coverchiefs ful fyne weren of ground;
I dorste swere they weyeden ten pound
That on a Sonday weren upon hir heed.
Hir hosen weren of fyn scarlet reed,
Ful streite yteyd, and of shoes ful moyste and / newe.
Boold was hir face, and fair, and reed of hewe.
She was a worthy womman al hir lyve:
Housbondes at chirche dore she hadde fyve,
Withouten oother compaignye in youthe –
But thereof nedeth nat to speke as nowthe.
And thries hadde she been at Jerusalem;
She hadde passed many a straunge strem;
At Rome she hadde been, and at Boloigne,
In Galice at Seint-Jame, and at Coloigne.
She koude muchel of wandrynge by the weye.
Gat-tothed was she, soothly for to seye.
Upon an amblere esily she sat,

Ywympled wel, and on hir heed an hat
As brood as is a bokeler or a targe;
A foot-mantel aboute hir hipes large,
And on hir feet a paire of spores sharpe.
In felaweshipe wel koude she laughe and carpe.
Of remedies of love she knew per chaunce,
For she koude of that art the olde daunce.

(1(A), ll.445–76)

Once again physical description is important. The Wife wears headcoverings of the finest texture, huge and elaborate affairs. Her carefully laced stockings are red, her shoes of the newest, most supple leather decorated with spurs. Her large hat is as broad as a shield and her wimple almost covers her face. She wears a 'foot-mantel', an overskirt like an apron, over her wide hips. We are told that she is fair, bold of face with a fresh 'reed' complexion and a gap in her front teeth. She is also rather deaf, a seemingly insignificant factor that might be relevant to her story later on.

Other details are noted. She is a cloth-maker so well reputed that she is said to surpass the finest in Belgium. She is well travelled having been on several pilgrimages already, some abroad, and apparently religious, always first up to the altar to offer at Mass. Thus she seems to be a striking woman, an ostentatious character, not young, a prosperous widow several times over. The signs of her wealth are there for all to see.

How far do other details undercut this portrait? We are told that the Wife was 'a worthy womman al hir lyve', a fact immediately set against the next line in which it is said that she has been married five times. The idea that this is simple misfortune is slyly dispelled in the additional remark about her liking for male company, the 'oother compaignye in youthe'. Here, the narrator breaks off as though this is irrelevant for it 'nedeth nat to speke as nowthe', but, cleverly, the damage has already been done and suspicions aroused. That this is a woman of some appetite is further indicated by the fact that she is 'Gat-tothed', a revealing detail of physiognomy for a medieval audience. Similarly she is bold of face and in her dress, her shocking red stockings almost matching her high complexion. She is associated with the vibrant colour red, itself an indication of heat and lasciviousness.

At the end of this passage there is once again a sudden switch to an apparently unconnected detail. It is said that she loves company in which she can laugh and chatter. In addition, 'per chaunce' – a remark suggesting this is not important, a sure sign that it is – she knows lots of remedies for love while she herself 'koude of that art the olde daunce'. This then is a woman of the world in every sense. She knows the tricks of her trade, cloth-making, and the tricks of the trade in love and marriage in which she has had plenty of practice. The Wife likes to draw attention to herself and her prosperity. She is far from shy, a larger-than-life character proud of her skills and her wealth, a loud and dominant personality. Everything about her is large, from her body, her broad hips, to her huge head-covering amusingly weighing, 'I dorste swere', ten pounds! We get the impression too that social standing is important to her. Though she is always the first up to the altar, this is mainly for show, an idea hinted at in the casual aside that if someone beats her to it

'so wrooth was she
That she was out of alle charitee.'

So, physical appearance is extremely important once more along with additional reference to occupation and pastimes or personal habits. On the one hand, the Wife is an amusing, vibrant, dominating character. At the same time, details accumulate and other seemingly meaningless remarks point to the depiction of an almost frightening, sexually voracious character who is all show. Which is she? Does her individual poem offer any further clues? This is a question to which we will return later.

The next extract in this section centres upon the opening description of Nicholas in the *Miller's Tale*.

This clerk was cleped hende Nicholas.
Of deerne love he koude and of solas;
And therto he was sleigh and ful privee,
And lyk a mayden meke for to see.
A chambre hadde he in that hostelrye
Allone, withouten any compaignye,
Ful fetisly ydight with herbes swoote;

And he hymself as sweete as is the roote
Of lycorys, or any cetewale.
His Almageste, and his bookes grete and smale,
His astrelabie, longynge for his art,
His augrym stones layen faire apart,
On shelves couched at his beddes heed;
His presse ycovered with a faldyng reed;
And al above ther lay a gay sautrie,
On which he made a-nyghtes melodie
So swetely that all the chambre rong;
And *Angelus ad virginem* he song;
And after that he song the Kynges Noote.
Ful often blessed was his myrie throte.
And thus this sweete clerk his tyme spente
After his freendes fyndyng and his rente.

(1(A), ll.3199–220)

Here, surprisingly, there is no real reference to physical appearance or details of clothing. Instead, his possessions are listed, his personality described, and his activities carefully noted. Though the details are different, the technique remains the same. Do individual features accumulate to present a subtly different picture from the one formed by an initial reading? In fact, your suspicions might already have been aroused by the way in which physical appearance is largely ignored and other personal characteristics favoured.

At first, Nicholas seems meekly innocent, 'lyk a mayden', a poor student interested in study, his learning evident from the books and other paraphernalia neatly arranged in his room. He has a marvellous singing voice too, is sweetly fragrant, is described as 'hende', a courteous and apparently most pleasant young man. Yet, once again, there is a hidden subtlety in this passage, the same word 'hende' set against the remark that he is also 'sleigh and ful privee', a secretive sly fellow constantly in search not of knowledge but of 'solas' and 'deerne love', a discreet sexual satisfaction. His room is artfully arranged, more as a pretence to learning, to false knowledge, than its actual pursuit. In pride of place is not the precious book that might be expected but his 'gay sautrie', his nights devoted to its playing, accompaniment to his lovely singing. Here his intentions are subtly hinted at. Though Nicholas sings the *Angelus*, he is another would-be courtly lover, scented by herbs, his voice an attraction with which to capture the women he desires. Like Absolon he admires a pretty face but, unlike his later rival, it is clear that Nicholas's love is far from idealised gazing from afar; carnal 'solas' is his aim.

Earlier we saw that it was the cumulative effect of details that revealed Absolon to his audience. Here the technique is slightly different; this time it is the *juxtaposition* of details that is crucial. Just as Absolon's liking for taverns and jolly barmaids was set against his squeamish loathing of coarse speech or 'fartyng', Nicholas is surrounded by the trappings of learning yet spends his time chasing women. In each case, the animalistic and the intellectual are juxtaposed. Sly asides undercut initial impressions. Here the opening line is set against the following three. In a similar manner, individual words are associated with Nicholas and repeated with increasing irony, their use designed to draw attention to the exact opposite of what they seem to suggest. Nicholas is described as 'sweete', as in fragrant, then, later the reader is told that he sings so 'swetely'. At the end he is 'this sweete clerk'. Yet, now that a fuller picture has emerged, this is only what he *appears* to be. Such words or phrases continue to be associated with him throughout the poem, 'hende' being one example. Look out for this in other portraits, and examine too how the repetition of key words or phrases modifies our initial impression and thus contributes to Chaucer's use of irony.

Further analysis of the poem as a whole indicates that impressions of characters prepare the ground for the development of plot. Again, an extract from the *Miller's Tale* offers some important clues. Here, Nicholas prepares to take advantage of old John's absence to seduce his young wife. As you read this, think back to the earlier description of Nicholas and ask yourself whether this extract confirms our first impression of him. You might also focus upon the ways in which this second picture prepares for his successful wooing of Alison and hoaxing of John the carpenter.

> Now, sire, and eft, sire, so bifel the cas,
> That on a day this hende Nicholas
> Fil with this yonge wyf to rage and pleye,

Whil that hir housbonde was at Oseneye,
As clerkes ben ful subtile and ful queynte;
And prively he caughte hire by the queynte,
And seyde, 'Ywis, but if ich have my wille,
For deerne love of thee, lemman, I spille.'
And heeld hire harde by the haunchebones,
And seyde, 'Lemman, love me al atones,
Or I wol dyen, also God me save!'
And she sproong as a colt dooth in the trave,
And with hir heed she wryed faste awey,
And seyde, 'I wol nat kisse thee, by my fey!
Why, lat be!' quod she. 'Lat be, Nicholas,
Or I wol crie "out harrow" and "allas"!
Do wey youre handes, for youre curteisye!'
  This Nicholas gan mercy for to crye,
And spak so faire, and profred him so faste,
That she hir love hym graunted atte laste,
And swoor hir ooth, by Seint Thomas of Kent,
That she wol been at his comandement,
Whan that she may hir leyser wel espie.
'Myn housbonde is so ful of jalousie
That but ye wayte wel and been privee,
I woot right wel I nam but deed,' quod she.
'Ye moste been ful deerne, as in this cas.'
  'Nay, therof care thee noght,' quod Nicholas.
'A clerk hadde litherly biset his whyle,
But if he koude a carpenter bigyle.'
And thus they been accorded and ysworn
To wayte a time, as I have told biforn.
  Whan Nicholas had doon thus everideel
And thakked hire aboute the lendes weel,
He kiste hire sweete and taketh his sawtrie,
And pleyeth faste, and maketh melodie.

(1(A), ll.3271–306)

Immediately several details are striking. Once again he is termed 'hende' Nicholas. This is a man so courteous and *courtly*, so much the idealising lover adoring his love-object, Alison, that he grabs her at the first opportunity, as soon as the coast is clear, so he can 'rage and pleye'. Without doubt, he knows how to play the lover. He begs for 'mercy' and 'spak so faire'. He presses his suit, 'profred him so faste', claiming that he will die for love of her. He takes too his 'sawtrie' and 'pleyeth faste' using this lovely melody as a means to woo her, or so the closing lines reveal.

Yet Nicholas has already succeeded with this young woman, and with some ease too. Juxtaposed against his fine words and musical accomplishment is the fact that he is a physical lover under no illusions about what he wants; he desires his 'wille'. Again there is a reference to 'deerne' love for which he fears he will 'spille', a sexual innuendo punning on the verb 'to die'. Nicholas calls her 'lemman', a very ordinary endearment and holds her hard by the thighs while, later, he 'thakked hire aboute the lendes weel', intimately strokes and caresses her. Alison herself implies that his hands are everywhere when she urges 'Do wey youre handes, for youre curteisye!' Perhaps the most telling detail occurs early on when just as he is about to murmur elegant words of love Nicholas grasps her 'by the queynte', an extremely graphic and coarse detail offset against his cunning sweet-talk.

On the surface their pact appears to be a courtly promise. Alison agrees to save him from death by returning his love, indicated by the elegant terms used as she 'graunted' him his wish, 'swoor' she would be 'at his comandement' in an echo of Nicholas's own courtly language. But Alison knows full well that this is a purely physical and adulterous liaison. She simply asks that he wait until her jealous husband offers them a chance for 'deerne' love. She appears too to enjoy the game. Though she twists away and pretends that she won't kiss him, it remains fun and so 'she sproong as a colt', an ambiguous simile both suggesting that Alison is young, innocent and skittish, and also indicating a base, animalistic earthiness. That, like Nicholas, she remains a down-to-earth character is seen in her frequent oaths. Everything remains an enjoyable game so that in the closing lines of this passage, Nicholas expresses the idea that it will be easy to fool a simple carpenter.

Thus it is suggested that Nicholas's depiction as a sly cunning fellow only after one thing is an accurate one and here he finds a willing companion in such sport. What seems to make Nicholas so successful is his ability to marry hard physical lust with clever courteous words, indicated by the technique of juxtaposing the language of courtly love with details of his physical pursuit. In this way Nicholas is contrasted with the hints given to us earlier about Absolon, and the narrative prepares for the way in which John is about to be duped. At this point the tale is already moving on apace with the main characters introduced and their relationships beginning to be established. Earlier, signs of Nicholas's apparent learning were brought to our notice and it is known that he is cunning. If John's depiction as a gullible old fool is accurate, how do you anticipate Nicholas will trick him? The narrator of this story has already set up the outcome in other ways too. Notice how he refers back to the agreement to wait for a more suitable time 'as I have told biforn'. You might also have spotted that hints about courtly love and the idea of ignorance set against learning tend to keep occurring now, suggesting something about Chaucer's themes and interests, a matter to which I shall return in Chapter 4.

The final extract in this section is taken from the point at which Alison and Nicholas finally spend the night together while John is away. As you read it focus upon the following questions:

What are you expecting to happen now? In what ways might Absolon and Nicholas be contrasted and how might this be important in terms of plot?

Whan that the firste cok hath crowe, anon
Up rist this joly lovere Absolon,
And hym arraieth gay, at poynt-devys.
But first he cheweth greyn and lycorys,
To smellen sweete, er he hadde kembd his heer.
Under his tonge a trewe-love he beer,
For therby wende he to ben gracious.
He rometh to the carpenteres hous,
And stille he stant under the shot-wyndowe –
Unto his brest it raughte, it was so lowe –
And softe he cougheth with a semy soun:
'What do ye, hony-comb, sweete Alisoun,
My faire bryd, my sweete cynamome?
Awaketh, lemman myn, and speketh to me!
Wel litel thynken ye upon my wo,

That for youre love I swete ther I go.
No wonder is tho that I swelte and swete;
I moorne as dooth a lamb after the tete.
Ywis, lemman, I have swich love-longynge
That lik a turtel trewe is my moornynge.
I may nat ete na moore than a mayde.'
   'Go fro the wyndow, Jakke fool,' she sayde;
'As help me God, it wol nat be "com pa me".
I love another – and elles I were to blame –
Wel bet than thee, by Jhesu, Absolon.
Go forth thy wey, or I wol caste a ston,
And lat me slepe, a twenty devel wey!'
   'Allas,' quod Absolon, 'and weylawey,
That trewe love was evere so yvel biset!
Thanne kysse me, syn it may be no bet,
For Jhesus love, and for the love of me.'
   'Wiltow thanne go thy wey therwith?' quod / she.
   'Ye, certes, lemman,' quod this Absolon.
   'Thanne make thee redy,' quod she, 'I come / anon.'
And unto Nicholas she seyde stille,
'Now hust, and thou shalt laughen al thy fille.'
   This Absolon doun sette hym on his knees
And seyde, 'I am a lord at alle degrees;
For after this I hope ther cometh moore.
Lemman, thy grace, and sweete bryd, thyn / oore!'

(1(A), ll.3687–726)

Earlier extracts suggested how a vaguely effeminate Absolon thought he was a courtly lover, carefully preening and adorning himself. Here this prettified 'joly lovere' gets up at first light to ensure that he is handsomely dressed 'at poynt-devys', right down to the last detail. He chews cardamom and liquorice to sweeten his breath. His hair is carefully combed. Under his tongue he places 'a trewe-love', a four-leafed sprig of herbs in the shape of a love-knot. In this way, we are told, he hopes 'to ben gracious' or attractive. He positions himself with care beneath the low, hinged window. The details of this window's height are carefully recorded for this is obviously going to be important in terms of plot and will enable the 'lovers' to reach each other. Absolon stands there like a troubadour and prepares to croon his words of love.

His initial portrait failed to mention his actual success rate with the ladies. Unlike Nicholas, it seems that he is no 'deerne' lover able to woo Alison with courtly words yet engage in rough and tumble love play. It comes as no surprise then to find that he attempts to sway Alison by his eloquence alone. Having already seen that this is unlikely to win her affections, the reader is prepared for her rejection of him.

Absolon's choice of words is highly amusing. He quietly clears his throat before launching into what we immediately recognise is a prepared speech. His language is full of endearments such as 'sweete Alisoun', 'hony-comb', 'My faire bryd, my sweete cynamome', 'sweete bryd', and, of course, the more prosaic 'lemman' which makes a frequent appearance. He tells of his apparently idealised yearning for her declaring

> 'I have swich love-longynge
> That lik a turtel trewe is my moornynge.'

He claims that he can scarcely eat for love of her and cries 'allas' that true love was 'evere so yvel biset!' He begs for one kiss and when Alison agrees, only if he will then leave her alone, declares himself a 'lord' in every way. He also calls for his beloved's 'grace' and 'oore'.

Absolon mingles the highly stylised language of courtly love with the prosaic and hence his actions are extremely entertaining. Love-longing makes him 'swelte and swete', an idea repeated in the following line. This is hardly an attractive or desirable attribute in a lover! At the same time, he claims 'I moorne as dooth a lamb after the tete', an intimation of his more basic desire as well as an amusing simile that merely makes him appear plaintive and feeble. Absolon, unlike his rival in love, simply seems unable to get it right.

This then is the comic picture that greets the earthy Alison as she is woken at the crack of dawn after a night in bed with her expert, lusty lover Nicholas. Her reply is hardly unexpected after the careful way in which these character portraits have been established and embellished, but it remains highly entertaining. It is easy to imagine Absolon's quavering little voice recounting his love sickness, attempting to ape the courtly lover he thinks Alison will admire. Her answer is a total contrast to this sort of approach and has the effect of bathos, of suddenly bringing everything down to earth as she cries 'Go fro the wyndow, Jakke fool'. She refuses to embrace him, an insistence couched in the uncouth 'com pa me', or 'come kiss me'. She tells him she loves another and, to compound Absolon's disappointment, leaves him in no doubt that his rival surpasses him in every way:

> 'I love another – and elles I were to blame –
> Wel bet than thee, by Jhesu, Absolon.'

Where he swears his love for her on Christ, she uses the oath in an altogether more basic manner.

Alison tells him to clear off and let her sleep or she will resort to the physical – in contrast to his fine words – and throw a stone at him, an amusing remark intensified by Absolon's inadequate attempt to keep the proceedings fixed on a more spiritual level:

> 'Allas,' quod Absolon, 'and weylawey,
> That trewe love was evere so yvel biset!'

Somewhat surprisingly, however, he remains insistent, and it is here that some earlier hints are gathered up and made explicit. Though Absolon does not engage in the sort of horse play so admired by Alison and at which Nicholas is so adept, preferring instead to believe that sweet talk alone will do the trick, his intentions remain the same. It was noted earlier that he had sweetened his breath and deliberately positioned himself at the window at a height more convenient for reaching his beloved. He plans a kiss at the very least, and when Alison agrees to this he prepares himself with care. On his knees, begging 'thyn oore', he appears the perfect, subservient lover. Yet, he himself declares 'after this I hope ther cometh moore'.

The plot thickens as the audience realise he is going to get more than he bargained for. He seems oblivious to the fact that Alison is clearly resistant to his imagined charms. He is certainly unaware that not only has she Nicholas in the room beside her, but she is preparing to play a practical joke on him, urging Nicholas to keep quiet 'and thou shalt laughen al thy fille'. It might be interesting to read on and explore the ways in which this passage – with its carefully noted details, its use of language, and cleverly manipulated contrasts – prepares the audience for the final humorous outcome.

Conclusion

What then has our exploration of these varying extracts revealed? What is immediately clear is that there is no one distinct or separate thing that constitutes Chaucer's style. Though several features might be important and easy to identify, it is the cumulative effect of these – the picture as a whole – that remains crucial. Successful characterisation is integral to each poem, however, whether involved with plot, themes or ideas, or highlighting the personalities of those speakers who will tell their own tales.

How has character been depicted so far? The following techniques, *in any combination*, have all been seen:

1. details of physical appearance
2. details of clothing
3. details of occupation
4. details of habits or ways in which time is spent
5. the use of colour as a symbol or representation of an idea (e.g. red).

These might be described as stylistic features or symbols.

Other techniques have also been revealed:

1. repetition of key words or phrases associated with a character.(e.g. 'hende')
2. *juxtaposition* of details (especially from the first list), the way features, events, or styles of language are contrasted or offset against each other.
3. the sort of language used particularly in direct speech. Not only *what* is said but *how* it is expressed might be important. (e.g. is it high and elaborately elegant or basic and down-to-earth in style?)

4. the narrator's casual remarks or additional inserted comments might help to reveal attitude towards characters as well as, indirectly, their personality traits.
5. many of these portraits have been deliberately humorous or ironic in tone where gathering up a series of contrasting or apparently irrelevant details might undercut first impressions. Irony might also be revealed in the cumulative effect of certain repeated details or key words and phrases.

On a general level, it has been seen that the ways in which characters behave and respond to each other is important especially in terms of plot outcome. Also, that first readings are usually qualified by closer ones. Perhaps the main thing learned is that Chaucer is a slippery writer, in that words or details may not always be what they first seem and final impressions remain ambiguous. When a character is presented through a series of totally contrasting views, which, if any, are final or definitive? Does it matter that sometimes this cannot be told? Reading *The Canterbury Tales* in an open-ended way, asking questions of the text and looking carefully for evidence to support your ideas, as exemplified in this first chapter, might be the most valuable approach.

Further Work

- Look at any portrait in the *General Prologue* and analyse it in the variety of ways used here. Then read the tale told by your chosen individual. Do they tell the tale you might have expected, or not? In what ways does it conform to your expectation or how is it different?
- Analyse the characters appearing in a poem of your choice. How far do the initial portraits prepare the reader for the plot ahead? Look too at the interaction of these characters especially the sort of language each uses. In what ways might this use of language be revealing?
- How does Chaucer prepare the audience for the events to come? How does the narrative unfold?

- Look at the ways in which humour is conveyed in either the description of a character or through the narrative or plot. To help, you might like to focus upon the sorts of techniques identified in this chapter.

II: OTHER STYLISTIC FEATURES – THE *NUN'S PRIEST'S TALE*, THE *PARDONER'S TALE*, AND THE *WIFE OF BATH'S PROLOGUE*

Characterisation and plot are obviously not Chaucer's only concerns. We have already seen the importance of humour and the use of dialogue and contrast – features discussed further in this section. Other stylistic techniques include the creation of fictional voices which have an effect upon the tales told as well as upon ways of telling them, and it is this technique in particular which is our focus in this section.

The first extract is taken from the *Nun's Priest's Tale* and occurs just after Chauntecleer has related details of a fearful dream in which he was attacked by a terrible animal in his own back yard. It is likely that his groans and moans of fear wake Pertelote to whom he recounts the dreadful details, building a picture of a fiend so awful that one look from it almost frightens Chauntecleer to death. It is in the light of this knowledge that you might like to consider Pertelote's response. How does Chaucer's fictional narrator make this passage amusing? What is Chaucer's intention in highlighting the features depicted here?

"Avoy!" quod she, "fy on yow, hertelees!
Allas!" quod she, "for, by that God above,
Now han ye lost myn herte and al my love!
I kan nat love a coward, by my feith!
For certes, what so any womman seith,
We alle desiren, if it myghte bee,
To han housbondes hardy, wise, and free,
And secree – and no nygard, ne no fool,
Ne hym that is agast of every tool,
Ne noon avauntour, by that God above!
How dorste ye seyn, for shame, unto youre love

That any thyng myghte make yow aferd?
Have ye no mannes herte, and han a berd?
Allas! And konne ye been agast of swevenys?
Nothyng, God woot, but vanitee in sweven is.
Swevenes engendren of replecciouns,
And ofte of fume and of complecciouns,
Whan humours been to habundant in a wight.
Certes this dreem, which ye han met to-nyght,
Cometh of the greete superfluytee
Of youre rede colera, pardee,
Which causeth folk to dreden in hir dremes
Of arwes, and of fyr with rede lemes,
Of rede beestes, that they wol hem byte,
Of contek, and of whelpes, grete and lyte;
Right as the humour of malencolie
Causeth ful many a man in sleep to crie
For feere of blake beres, or boles blake,
Or elles blake develes wole hem take.
Of othere humours koude I telle also
That werken many a man sleep ful wo;
But I wol passe as lightly as I kan.
  "Lo Catoun, which that was so wys a man,
Seyde he nat thus, 'Ne do no fors of dremes'?
  "Now sire," quod she, "whan we flee fro the / bemes,
For Goddes love, as taak som laxatyf.
Up peril of my soule and of my lyf,
I conseille yow the beste – I wol nat lye –
That bothe of colere and of malencolye
Ye purge yow; and for ye shal nat tarie,
Though in this toun is noon apothecarie,
I shal myself to herbes techen yow
That shul been for youre hele and for youre / prow;
And in oure yeerd tho herbes shal I fynde
The whiche han of hire propretee by kynde
To purge yow bynethe and eek above.
Foryet nat this, for Goddes owene love!
Ye been ful coleryk of compleccioun;
Ware the sonne in his ascencioun
Ne fynde yow nat repleet of humours hoote.
And if it do, I dar wel leye a grote,

That ye shul have a fevere terciane,
Or an agu that may be youre bane.
A day or two ye shul have digestyves
Of wormes, er ye take youre laxatyves
Of lawriol, centaure, and fumetere,
Or elles of ellebor, that groweth there,
Of katapuce, or of gaitrys beryis,
Of herbe yve, growyng in oure yeerd, ther / mery is;

(VIII, ll.2908–66)

Chauntecleer's preceeding speech ended with the weak regular line and fill-in word 'doutelees' in a manner suggesting that his voice simply fades away. Pertelote's jeering response has the impact of sudden contrast, and immediately punctures her husband's imaginative musings. Her first word is an exclamation, 'Avoy!', while 'fy', 'Allas!', 'by that God above', and 'by my feith' are all packed into the first four lines. She speaks in plain and coarse language full of frequent oaths. She refers to 'that God above' or 'God woot', and later to God's love on more than one occasion. At the same time she showers her husband with insults, calling him 'hertelees' and a 'coward', and finally threatening 'Now han ye lost myn herte and al my love'. Twice Pertelote disrupts the metre; her use of 'fy' in the opening line emphasises her loud cry, while 'Now', which begins the third line of the extract, reverses the metre to give a tyrannical thump of dogmatism to her voice. What this opening gives us then is a sudden flurry of exclamations, an emphatic, disturbed rhythm, and a radical change of diction. All of these elements enable Chaucer to establish the power of Pertelote's voice.

Hers is a distinct voice which becomes more developed as her speech proceeds. The oaths, things like 'for Goddes owene love', are frequent. Other ideas are repeated so often that they are like a refrain. These include 'sweven', 'dreme', and their variants (repeated six times), and 'laxatyf', 'purge', 'digestyves' (five times). Her talk seems to keep returning to the same fixed ideas. This repetition, for example of 'sweven' and 'dreme', ensures that her thoughts are rambling rather than carefully developed. At the same time each mention of dreams strengthens her contempt until we are left with the feeling that she simply keeps on and on, wearing down the listener. This is reinforced by the way in which her questions and demands pile up (ll.2918–22 and 2943–57) in a verbal attack that permits no defence. Similarly her command that Chauntecleer take a 'laxatyf' is hammered home in a manner that effectively prevents him from objecting.

Apart from these repetitions, Pertelote's language seems to have two distinct strands. First, there are longer, more impressive terms from her medical superstitions and herb-lore. She uses words such as 'repleccciouns', 'compleccciouns', 'habundant' and 'superfluytee' from medicine, as well as mentioning herbs such as 'lawriol, centaure, and fumetere', 'ellebor', and 'katapuce'. Some of these are ridiculous, like the pretentious 'repleccciouns' for 'over-eating', and suggest that she is duped by the doctor's long words. Secondly, natural earthy language appears in simple, common words such as 'whelpes', 'grote', 'agu', and 'wormes', as well as in her colloquial constructions. Her quotation from Cato is particularly funny, her 'ne do no fors of' being roughly equivalent to 'don't take no notice of' in modern English.

Some of Pertelote's sentences also contribute to the humorous and forceful contrast between her speech and Chauntecleer's previous one. Their long and rambling construction suggests a nagging, seemingly endless tirade. This happens when she describes her ideal man as a strong, wise, tough husband, one who is 'secree' or discreet, not a 'niggard' or a miser, one who is neither a fearful 'fool' nor a boaster or 'avauntour'. Her description conforms to the commonly held ideal of a masculine hero, but the structure of the sentence is loose, each phrase strung onto a comma and conjunctions like 'and' or 'ne', as if she carelessly tacks on more ideas, one after another, rather than stop talking. Two interjections ('what so any womman seith' and 'if it myghte be') add to this garrulous effect. We find other examples of these nagging sentences when Pertelote enlarges on the idea of 'youre rede colera' (ll.2926–32), and when she lists her remedial herbs (ll.2961–6). The effect of this diction is to present the voice of a superstitious and vulgar Pertelote haranguing her husband.

Chaucer has characterised her richly then, and the tone of her voice makes us laugh. However, if we look at the argument she puts forward, we can see that there is a serious dispute, a real difference of character, between her and Chauntecleer.

Pertelote's words present her practical common sense in opposition to Chauntecleer's masculine authority. How, she asks, can anyone fear dreams, and her common sense seems to deflate entirely Chauntecleer's self-important description of his nightmare. The effect is a bathetic one puncturing the picture given earlier, making it seem exaggerated and even silly. She declares that God knows there is nothing but vanity in dreams or 'swevenes'. This reference to God (and, amusingly, her swearing by God) draws attention to the fact that this is common knowledge supported by the ultimate, the highest authority, God, that no one can challenge.

She begins her dismissal of dreams by stating a simple prosaic cause for them: 'replecciouns' or over-eating. In addition they might be stimulated by the misalignment of bodily functions, by 'fume', or by an imbalance of bodily fluids or 'humours', believed by medieval people to fix personalities or dispositions. Chauntecleer's dream is analysed as stemming from an excess of his red choleric humour which stimulates fearful dreams of attack, of 'contek' or strife, of dreadful dogs, red flames, red beasts. In the same way a melancholic humour promotes frightening dreams centred on the colour black.

Pertelote's analysis is a straightforward explanation of Chauntecleer's fear. In one fell swoop her focus upon the body, upon the physiological causes of dreams, refutes Chauntecleer's imaginative description and, by implication, denudes dreaming of any psychological aspect. Thus she urges her husband to attach no importance to his dream, and in one abrupt phrase bluntly advises him to 'taak som laxatyf' in a humorous attempt to persuade him to purge his body because – as she has already reasoned – this will purge his over-stuffed mind as well. Everything is reduced to the level of the mundane, the physical.

At the same time Pertelote offers her own knowledge as authority, one based on personal experience, on tried and tested lore, in 'I conseille yow the beste – I wol nat lye'. Knowing him full of choleric humour, she offers her own folk wisdom, telling him which herbs are safe to eat if he is to 'purge yow bynethe and eek above'. She warns him to look after his health, to beware the midday sun, and to avoid overheating which will make him physically ill as well as fever his brain. She urges him to take other 'alternative' medicines to aid his digestion – worms, various foul-tasting herbs and berries. She offers natural homoeopathic remedies to cure what she believes is a physical problem. She argues here that it is personal, practical experience that is important, and not the more abstract and masculine authority of dreams, books, or famous authors.

Her argument is on the side of the prosaic set against the poetic, the everyday against the fanciful. Perhaps Chaucer is mocking his own role as a writer reliant on imagination or a Muse; certainly many of his narrators are inspired by dreams to recount their stories. With neat irony Pertelote even quotes 'Catoun' as an authority said to dismiss dreaming as a significant activity, though she cannot be sure that this is what he said. Dreams, like writing, were invested with masculine power; here Pertelote cites a masculine author as her own authority, though the suggestion is that she does so inaccurately. As we have already observed, the contrast between Chauntecleer's heightened, imaginative description of the dream-beast, and Pertelote's coarse, dismissive response, is extremely funny and designed to bring Chauntecleer down to earth with a bump.

You could set this passage against his lengthy reply where he cites dream lore and a seemingly endless list of authors and authorities in a contrasting ideal. What is Chaucer's intent here? Do you think he is exposing the gulf between ideal and practical perceptions of life in this comic interchange? We know from Chauntecleer's dream that the 'ideal' side of this issue is presented via his self-importance and imaginative exaggeration. Our analysis of Pertelote's voice shows that, in contrast, Chaucer overlays the 'practical' with a comic mix of superstition, coarse vulgarity and credulity. Who then, if anyone, speaks the most sense? How does the outcome of this debate – the fact that Chauntecleer's dream is finally prophetic – modify Chaucer's theme?

Our second extract, also from the *Nun's Priest's Tale*, is a further example of how humour is created. It also involves the direct intervention of the tale's narrator who is busy preparing for the climactic scene when Chauntecleer's dream comes true and he is so nearly tricked by the fox. As you read it, try to keep the following questions in your mind. First, it is the description of Chauntecleer and the details of his environment which are the source of humour here: what do you notice about them? Second, what is the effect of the narrator's style of telling this tale?

A col fox, ful of sly iniquitee,
That in the grove hadde woned yeres three,
By heigh ymaginacioun forncast,
The same nyght thurghout the hegges brast
Into the yerd ther Chauntecleer the faire
Was wont, and eek his wyves, to repaire;
And in a bed of wortes stille he lay
Til it was passed undren of the day,
Waitynge his tyme on Chauntecleer to falle,
As gladly doon thise homycides alle
That in await liggen to mordre men.
O false mordrour, lurkynge in thy den!
O newe Scariot, newe Genylon,
False dissymulour, o Greek Synon,
That broghtest Troye al outrely to sorwe!
O Chauntecleer, acursed be that morwe
That thou into that yerd flaugh fro the bemes!
Thou were ful wel ywarned by thy dremes
That thilke day was perilous to thee;
But what that God forwoot moot nedes bee,
After the opinioun of certein clerkis.
Witnesse on hym that any parfit clerk is,
That in scole is greet alteracioun
In this mateere, and greet disputisoun,
And hath been of an hundred thousand men.
But I ne kan nat bulte it to the bren
As kan the hooly doctour Augustyn,
Or Boece, or the Bisshop Bradwardyn,
Wheither that Goddes worthy forwityng
Streyneth me nedely for to doon a thyng –
"Nedely" clepe I symple necessitee –
Or elles, if free choys be graunted me
To do that same thyng, or do it noght,
Though God forwoot it er that I was wroght;
Or of his wityng streyneth never a deel

But by necessitee condicioneel.
I wol nat han to do of swich mateere;
My tale is of a cok, as ye may heere,
That tok his conseil of his wyf, with sorwe,
To walken in the yerd upon that morwe
That he hadde met that dreem that I yow tolde.
Wommennes conseils been ful ofte colde;
Wommannes conseil broghte us first to wo
And made Adam fro Paradys to go,
Ther as he was ful myrie and wel at ese.
But for I noot to whom it myght displese,
If I conseil of wommen wolde blame,
Passe over, for I seyde it in my game.

(VIII, ll.3215–62)

Earlier the Nun's Priest described Chauntecleer as royal, courtly, master of all he surveys, the finest example of his kind with his seven wives and loud crow. This glowing praise prepares the audience for his fall, for the bathetic effect we saw in the preceding extract, and to which the narrator now adds. There is, however, a wider issue hinted at here, one introduced by the Nun's Priest's comment made just before this section, that his story is as true as the romance tale of Lancelot and Guinevere, so well loved by women. What is he hinting at here? Can a romance be true? Is it to be recommended if women in particular are said to like it? On the one hand we are prepared for an epic tale of heroic exploits and yet at the same time its 'truth' is called into question, thus preparing us for the humour to come as well as touching on attitudes to women to which we shall return in Chapter 4.

Let us first focus upon the way in which this tale is narrated. Chauntecleer continues to be cast in the mould of the courtly hero. He is termed 'Chauntecleer, the faire' and deemed to be safe there in his kingdom, 'the yerd'. In contrast, the sly fox hides overnight in the cabbage patch. The details of his depiction indicate his cunning and his status as an outsider beyond the 'civilised' world. (He lives in the 'grove'.) The contrast also reminds us that this is a comic tale where the description of Chauntecleer as a romance hero is frankly ludicrous; he is simply a farmyard cockerel. Yet the narrator continues to inflate his story and turn it into a tale of chivalry.

The fox patiently bides his time ready for when his victim will 'falle'. Chauntecleer is made to seem like a worthy king or leader unwittingly awaiting his assassination. This idea is reinforced as we are told that the fox is like all murderers 'That in await liggen to mordre men'. The narrator warms to his theme inflating his tale until it resembles an ancient or classical fable. He achieves this effect in several ways.

First he uses the more impersonal pronoun 'thou' or 'thine' throughout, in contrast to the intimate and plain speech of the preceding passage where Pertelote speaks directly as an equal with 'yow' and 'ye'. Secondly he uses the apostrophe, initially to berate the fox, Chauntecleer's betrayer:

> 'O false mordrour, lurkynge in thy den!
> O newe Scariot, newe Genylon,
> False dissymulour, o Greek Synon. . . .'

The term 'lurkynge' emphasises sly treachery while the repetition of 'O' deliberately builds to the moment of attack. It is not really tension, for the outcome has been 'prophesied', but its effect is one of emotional pathos designed to create fear for the mighty warrior Chauntecleer and make us laugh.

At the same time the narrator rails against the fox in a tirade associating him with other well-known betrayers of men. He refers to Judas Iscariot, to Genylon the betrayer of the Knight Roland in a favourite contemporary romance, to the deceiver Synon said to be responsible for the fall of Troy. The Bible, romance, epic history – none compare to the case of a fox trying to eat a cockerel for his dinner! The effect remains, however, with Chauntecleer the noble victim and the audience highly entertained. Chauntecleer's heroic and tragic qualities are compounded in another apostrophe:

> 'O Chauntecleer, acursed be that morwe
> That thou into that yerd flaugh fro the bemes!'

This seems to indicate that one single action is the key to his downfall as in the case of so many heroes who fall victim to destiny. If only he hadn't done it, the narrator suggests, a cry reinforced by another technique employed in these lines, the use of exclamation. (You probably recognised it earlier in 'O false mordrour, lurkynge in thy den!')

The part played by chance in the fall of the epic or romance hero is an important one. Scores of tales tell how if only the habits of a lifetime had been broken (in this case that Chauntecleer had stayed on the beams safely roosting out of reach), if only warnings had been heeded, or free will exercised, then a predestined fate could have been avoided. Thus the Nun's Priest ensures that the cockerel is cast as an heroic figure in a mock epic by adopting a further technique, reference to foreknowledge. Chauntecleer's dream warns that this particular day is 'perilous to thee'. The narrator notes that some clerks suggest that God's plan cannot be altered (ll.3234–5). Others disagree so that in this matter there exists 'greet disputisoun', involving learned authority figures such as Boethius, St Augustine, or Thomas Bradwardyne.

The Nun's Priest's interruption is a lengthy one at this point. On the one hand the citation of authorities and learned consideration of this feature of his chosen genre is yet another means of inflating the style of his tale, giving it a substance and importance it does not really possess, and so adding to the humour. Equally, however, the digression invites us to consider the question of free will itself, to consider the suggestion that if God has 'foreknowledge', has planned an event, then is it certain to happen, or can the exercise of choice or free will ensure its avoidance even if it has been predestined by God since before you were born? (ll.3245–50) The narrator speaks directly declaring himself unable to sort out the arguments: 'I ne kan nat bulte it to the bren.' What is the point of his interruption here? He leaves unresolved a debate designed to humorously underscore the mock-extraordinary nature of his narrative, but his own (fictional) voice also draws attention to an unanswered issue of Chaucer's time, one with which some of his poems at least partially engage.

The Nun's Priest takes great care to inflate his style in the ways we have just seen. What then are we to make of his next interruption, his reminder that 'My tale is of a cok, as ye may heere', one who reluctantly takes the advice of his wife, walks in the yard, ignoring his dream, and so meets his fate? Here this almost tongue-in-cheek aside totally deflates the mock-epic just created, and once again its effect is a bathetic one as audience and characters are brought down to earth by his timely reminder. At the same time the narrator's second digression seems to permit an opportunity to offer an anti-feminist opinion in the guise of a joking storyteller.

He notes that women's advice often proves if not fatal at least misguided, in support citing biblical authority blaming Eve for the Fall of Man and expulsion from the bliss of the Garden of Eden. He openly admits his fear of insulting some members of his audience and claims that all was said 'in my game' as a joke. He is only repeating his story, Chauntecleer's story, and so advises us to read written, and by implication, higher, authorities on the subject.

What is your reaction to this interlude? This is a narrator who uses authority to humorously lend weight to his tale. Here he uses it to support a view that he at once withdraws. Do you think he is joking or does his remark open up the question of reliance upon written authority? What is Chaucer's intention in creating this character, one whose voice tells his tale effectively and humorously? If you recall, in the first extract we examined, Pertelote set her own home-spun wisdom and lived experience against her husband's faith in dream lore and its explication by masculine written authority. Is there a connection here?

I would suggest that narrative and narrative style work on two levels. On the first, it is a means of successfully narrating a tale in a chosen manner using techniques and contrasts to enhance its telling. On the second, that same style, together with issues raised by the purpose of narratorial intervention, might be used to open up, to question, subvert, or slant a whole range of issues raised by Chaucer in his work. In this story he might be said to be considering the question of knowledge, of anti-feminism, even the problem of writing itself where nothing is ever quite 'truth', nothing can be read as a definitive or final authority. Already these stories can be seen as slippery, their narrative techniques part of an interrelated pattern.

Perhaps our later extract from the Wife of Bath exemplifies this more clearly. Just before we explore this however, let us take a look at a piece from near the start of the *Pardoner's Tale.* How effectively does the Pardoner use rhetorical devices in this short extract?

> Lo, how that dronken Looth, unkyndely,
> Lay by his doghtres two, unwityngly;
> So dronke he was, he nyste what he wroghte.
> Herodes, whoso wel the stories soghte,
> Whan he of wyn was repleet at his feeste,
> Right at his owene table he yaf his heeste
> To sleen the baptist John, ful giltelees.
> Senec seith a good word douteless;
> He seith he kan no difference fynde
> Bitwix a man that is out of his mynde
> And a man which that is dronkelewe,
> But that woodnesse, yfallen in a shrewe,
> Persevereth lenger than doth dronkenesse.
> O glotonye, ful of cursednesse!
> O cause first of oure confusioun!
> O original of oure dampnacioun,
> Til Crist hadde boght us with his blood agayn!
> Lo, how deere, shortly for to sayn,
> Aboght was thilke cursed vileynye!
> Corrupt was al this world for glotonye.

(VI (C), ll.485–504)

The Pardoner opens his tale with an indication that the three young men central to his story are debauched rioters guilty of the sins of blasphemy, lechery and gluttony, and drunkenness. This extract forms a small part of his lengthy introduction to the events of his fiction, a prologue that establishes his tale as a sermon, a vehicle solely intended for preaching against the horrors he outlines here.

His statement is bald and uncompromising, authorised by 'hooly writ', that wine and drunken behaviour lead to lechery. Our extract follows on from this clear teaching. The Pardoner immediately moves to offer biblical evidence for his words. 'Lo', he cries, 'look!' at how that drunken father Lot 'Lay by his doghtres two' without even realising it, an unnatural act prompted by the fact that 'So dronke he was, he nyste what he wroghte'. This is succeeded by a further well-known biblical example, that of Herod, recorded in 'the stories' or narratives of the gospels, who became so drunk at one of his own feasts that 'Right at his owene table' he vowed to slay John the Baptist, an innocent man, one 'ful giltelees', or so the Pardoner reminds us in an attempt to emphasise the appalling nature of this crime. Not content with this, he cites other written authority, the 'good word' of Seneca who claims that there is little difference between a drunkard and a madman except that madness lasts longer.

The Pardoner offers these comments as concrete examples to illustrate his preaching. These authorities are so well-known that they have the appearance of truth or fact, while the use of more than one is designed to expand and reinforce his teaching, ensuring that his 'lewed' audience receive the message. That his first two citations are so extreme as to be almost implausible is an irrelevancy. The crimes 'committed' while under the influence of drink are heinous ones and have the added weight of biblical authority. It is an authority which is cleverly utilised in the second half of the passage.

The Pardoner is a highly skilled orator who uses a mixture of abrupt and unequivocal statement, short examples or mini-stories such as the reference to Herod or Lot, and written learned authority, like Seneca, to clarify teaching points. At the same time he carefully punctuates his address with cries of 'Lo, how that dronken Looth' or 'Lo, how deere...', verbal flags or signals designed to retain interest and move on the pace of his narrative, as well as stirring and extravagant rhetorical tricks like the use of apostrophe or exclamation seen in the closing lines of the extract. Brief and to the point is the Pardoner's maxim. He offers three examples to 'prove' his teaching. Here he repeats the number, determined to retain his audience's involvement; he cries 'O glotonye, ful of cursednesse!', 'O cause first of oure' ruin, 'O original of oure dampnacioun'. Swiftly, almost without anyone noticing, the Pardoner equates 'dronkenesse' with the worse sin of 'glotonye' which is itself responsible for three things – 'cursednesse', our ruin, and original sin redeemed only by Christ's 'blood'.

It is a rhetorical trick involving a repetition of three seen throughout the opening to the *Pardoner's Tale*. At the same time his other techniques, including the use of apostrophe and exclamation, dramatically underline his point. That his tale has a moral or religious intent is without question. Skilfully his closing lines remind us that he is preaching against a wicked sin. That humans are prone to sinful behaviour is intimated in his remark about original sin, our expulsion from Paradise when Eve succumbed to temptation and offered the apple to Adam. It is an act redeemed only by Christ's death, something the Pardoner reiterates in his final exclamation as he reminds us of its terrible cost:

> 'Lo, how deere, shortly for to sayn,
> Aboght was thilke cursed vileynye!'

Thus what the Pardoner humorously terms the gluttony of Paradise (in effect merely the eating of an apple) has led to evil so that 'Corrupt was al this world for glotonye'. Using a range of rhetorical tricks to manipulate his audiences, he manages to induce a sense of guilt into them. The cunning and clever Pardoner is now ready to expand his theme, to deepen that guilt and, of course, to prepare for the real intent of his sermon-story which is not to preach against the sins nominated at the start, but to persuade his listeners to part with their money. As you read the remainder of his tale, be alert for the techniques and skills he uses in his pursuit of financial gain.

The Wife of Bath is often considered a problem voice in the *Tales*. What exactly is meant by this do you think? Here she attempts to tell of her numerous marriages presumably in order to disprove the clerical teachings she cites in the opening to her *Prologue*, and to offer her own experience (like Pertelote) as authority. She is just about to tell us of her most recent husband. What is the most striking thing about what she says here, or about the ways in which she does this? Like the Nun's Priest she digresses from her intended tale. What do you think this reveals?

> To chirche was myn housbonde born / a-morwe
> With neighebores, that for hym maden sorwe;
> And Jankyn, oure clerk, was oon of tho.
> As help me God, whan that I saugh hym go
> After the beere, me thoughte he hadde a paire

Of legges and of feet so clene and faire
That al myn herte I yaf unto his hoold.
He was, I trowe, twenty wynter oold,
And I was fourty, if I shal seye sooth;
But yet I hadde alwey a coltes tooth.
Gat-tothed I was, and that bicam me weel;
I hadde the prente of seinte Venus seel.
As help me God, I was a lusty oon,
And faire, and riche, and yong, and wel bigon,
And trewely, as myne housbondes tolde me,
I hadde the beste *quoniam* myghte be.
For certes, I am al Venerien
In feelynge, and myn herte is Marcien.
Venus me yaf my lust, my likerousnesse,
And Mars yaf me my sturdy hardynesse;
Myn ascendent was Taur, and Mars therinne.
Allas, allas! That evere love was synne!
I folwed ay myn inclinacioun
By vertu of my constellacioun;
That made me I koude noght withdrawe
My chambre of Venus from a good felawe.
Yet have I Martes mark upon my face,
And also in another privee place.
For God so wys be my savacioun,
I ne loved nevere by no discrecioun,
But evere folwede myn appetit,
Al were he short, or long, or blak, or whit;
I took no kep, so that he liked me,
How poore he was, ne eek of what degree.

(III (D), ll.593–626)

The Nun's Priest tends to interrupt his tale revealing only a few hints about his own character and directing our attention much more towards a series of questions or problems Chaucer leaves unanswered; the Wife doesn't so much interrupt her narrative as appear unable to get on with it. The introduction to her tale is a lengthy one apparently containing the story of her life. Yet even here she sometimes loses the thread of her narrative, while what she tells us is intensely revealing of her own personality. It is not simply that things have happened to her but that these events have shaped her. Hers is a voice that overshadows her tale. How then is her character displayed? Earlier we explored a series of techniques used by Chaucer to sketch his characters. Are any of them helpful here or is the Wife revealed to us in a different way?

Alison's is an emerging voice, one which appears by degrees through both the content of her speech and its style. She begins simply enough with a hint that her heart was set on Jankyn even before her previous husband had been decently buried. When her late husband is taken to church she tells us in an almost casual manner that it is her neighbours 'that for hym maden sorwe', not her. This telling omission is reinforced by her admission that she has eyes only for 'Jankyn, oure clerk', and her comment that she is unable to prevent herself looking at his lovely legs as he follows the funeral bier. Immediately this almost unseemly and shocking admission strikes home and we gain a strong sense of her energy and liveliness, indeed her frankly admitted sexuality. At the same time she informs her audience that she was forty years old when this occurred as opposed to Jankyn's twenty. What is the effect of these opening lines upon the reader? Are you amused, admiring, shocked, embarrassed? Perhaps almost regardless of your response the underlying feeling has to be one of curiosity – why should she wish to tell us these things? Her tone is intimate, one of confession, and you are drawn into it almost against your wishes.

Chaucer's depiction of this extremely lifelike figure continues as she now reveals herself further, totally forgetting that she was about to tell, in chronological order, of her series of marriages. Her focus is upon her own admission of her sexuality, part boastful perhaps, but also revealed with a sense of joy, in a manner that possibly forces you to revise your earlier impression of her. She declares that she has always had a 'coltes tooth'. Alison's youthful lustiness is indicated by her comments upon her own physiognomy. She remarks 'Gat-tothed I was', a sign of sexual appetite as is her strawberry-coloured birthmark, her 'seinte Venus seel' or 'Martes mark' found both on her face and in 'another privee place'. Here she is almost flirting, almost inviting you to check it out for yourself; her remarks certainly oblige her audience to recognise her for what she is.

Alison's sexuality is an openly declared one. She says 'As helpe me God, I was a lusty oon' and insists

> 'For certes, I am al Venerien
> In feelynge, and myn herte is Marcien'.

She is entirely aware of her own attributes, knows that she is lovely, rich, and in a good situation by virtue of being widowed; what is implicit here is a knowledge that marriage is based on more than love or lust, that factors like social standing and wealth are perhaps more likely to attract this young clerk than anything else she might offer, and it is this sharp awareness that begins to hint at something more than the amusing or even shocking impression she initially presents.

This hint is supported by the Wife's references to the planets. She indicates that she puts her trust in destiny, that all is predestined by astrology. It is not just that the planets with which she is associated, Venus and Mars, are suggestive of love and boldness. Alison's declaration is that this is simply her nature as she explains what each star sign gave her in the way of characteristics. When she says,

> 'I folwed ay myn inclinacioun
> By vertu of my constellacioun'

she leaves everything to astrology, suggests that nothing is under her control. In some senses she is excusing her own nature, revealing that such open sexuality might be considered shocking, even repugnant. She admits that she has never loved in moderation or 'by no discrecioun'. Instead her heart rules her head and she 'evere folwede myn appetit', taking no interest in whether the man concerned was old, young, rich, poor, black, white, tall, or short: 'I took no kep, so that he liked me'.

One reading of this confession is that Alison is a boastful, almost promiscuous character who enjoys embarrassing or shocking others, forcing her captive audience of pilgrims, who are expecting to hear her story, to listen to the lurid details of her love life. I would suggest, however, that this final quotation follows on from earlier hints that this amusing confession hides a deeper pain. Some of the details she has offered have been most intimate. She informs us that all her husbands have told her she has the 'beste *quoniam*' in town. Is this euphemism gross or endearing? What is perhaps important is that she is telling us of a moment when she has been praised or admired. Alison wants only to be loved. Her main concern is not the man himself; in one respect she is quite indiscriminate. Instead her feelings are aroused when, as the above quotation indicates, the man likes *her*. She sexually lavishes her own love on her men while her description of lusting after Jankyn's legs is as much adolescent infatuation as embarrassingly lustful. Her nature is brazen yet affectionate and loving; she tells us that despite her maturity and experience she falls head over heels for Jankyn, that 'al my herte I yaf unto his hoold'. Twice she tells us that she follows her sexual inclinations, adding that astrology is to blame; her remark is poignant in both its simplicity and given the nature of most medieval marriages. Alison is so loving that, as she says, she could never withhold 'My chambre of Venus from a good felawe'. Here is a woman who equates sex with love, or else one who recognises that love requires physical expression.

By the time the Wife reaches the line 'Allas, allas! That evere love was synne!' she is speaking from the heart, no longer a figure of fun or a monster. She craves a love that she has never really received (at least not until Jankyn), and her poignant cry reveals something of Chaucer's intention in creating a voice whose apparent inability to tell her story is more than merely comic. If the Nun's Priest's narratorial intervention hinted at the wider issues of his tale, is Chaucer using the fictional character of the Wife to open up questions concerning the function and practice of medieval marriage? Again this is an idea explored in Chapter 4.

Thus Chaucer builds this character with care. Almost unconsciously the Wife reveals herself. She digresses from her narrative, itself a hindrance to her actual tale. Several details have proved important; all need to be read in conjunction with each other. There is a strong sense of the confessional in this passage. That its real focus is her own self and not a 'story' of her marriage is clear from the frequent use of 'I', 'me' and 'myn'. At the same time there is a suggestion that Alison's mouth runs away with her as she prattles on almost oblivious of the effect she might be having on her audience. It is not just the frank details that indicate this but the sentence length or the phrases linked by numerous 'and's as in,

> 'As help me God, I was a lusty oon,
> And faire, and riche, and yong, and wel bigon,
> And trewely as myn housbondes told me,
> I hadde the beste *quoniam* myghte be.'

The lasting impression is of a voice that speaks from the heart, one shaped by its own rich experience.

Conclusion

The techniques explored in this second section build upon ones commented on earlier. Here it has been suggested that character is not simply revealed by the range delineated in our first discussions. Instead it is something more complex arising out of the movement and intention of the narrative itself, as in the *Nun's Priest's Tale*, out of the creation of a particularly powerful voice, as in the *Wife of Bath's Prologue*, and/or as part of a series of wider issues raised by the features of the narrative. Once again it is unlikely that any single approach will yield up the complexities of Chaucer's work, but it is possible to identify some of the features of style witnessed in these extracts. In your reading you might care to look out for the following:

1. The use of bathos – a prosaic response to deflate tension and bring a character or the proceedings down to earth. It usually relies heavily upon contrast with or juxtaposition to other 'set' pieces (so far the *Nun's Priest's Tale* and the *Miller's Tale*).
2. A high epic or heroic style – either used seriously or 'inflated' for comic effect as in the *Nun's Priest's Tale*. It incorporates some or all of the following:
   - citation of authorities, references to written, masculine sources

- use of exclamation
- use of apostrophe
- exaggerated or incongruous detail (See the *Nun's Priest's Tale*)
- reference to tragic or classical stories.

3. Narratorial intervention where the teller of a tale directly intervenes either to digress or remark on the proceedings, or ways of behaviour...Chaucer often uses this device to add humour or to make us question events or issues.
4. Revelation of speaker. Watch out for frequent use of personal pronouns ('I', 'myn', 'me'...) Its effect depends on both context and the tale being told. You will need to look closely at details, the structure of the passage, and its tone.
5. Sentence structure. We have particularly noticed looser, longer sentences where the speaker is carried away (Alison) or garrulous (Pertelote).

Further Reading

The style of the *Wife's Prologue* is intensely revealing. You might like to compare it with another 'problem' speaker, the Pardoner, to see how he discloses details about himself. Other tales involving much intervention by their tellers are the *Clerk's* and the *Man of Law's*. Similarly the use of authority as opposed to personal experience has been highlighted in the *Nun's Priest's* extracts. For further exploration, and in order to examine contrasting styles of story and speaker, read the tale of *Sir Thopas* (another send-up), the *Squire's* which is a romance, or the serious tale of *Melibee*. You may also wish to look again at the *Wife's Prologue*, this time at its opening where she sets clerical and scholarly authority against personal lived experience.

More generally, any tale of your choice would lend itself to an examination of style or speaker using the combination of techniques demonstrated in the second half of this chapter.

3

Voice, Narration and Form

I: THE DRAMATIC FRAME – THE MILLER, HARRY BAILLY AND CHAUCER-THE-PILGRIM

Who are the voices of *The Canterbury Tales*? A quick glance at any of the individual stories in the collection, particularly those most frequently set for study, indicates that each tale is told by a teller, the voice of a fictional narrator, one who is not Chaucer himself. It is a device which clearly has an effect upon the notion of tale telling as well as upon the issues each story raises. Within most tales there are two voices – Chaucer's and the fictional narrator's. Sometimes, as in the case of the *Nun's Priest's Tale*, there is more than one (Chauntecleer's, the fox's, Pertelote's). Equally some voices are 'louder' than others – the Wife's, the Pardoner's. Sometimes your set texts will include snippets suggesting the presence of other speakers, pilgrims involved in the story-telling contest devised and overseen by the Host, Harry Bailly, as indicated in the *General Prologue*. Then, of course, there is another character, the pilgrim who observes and narrates the proceedings, often referred to as Chaucer-the pilgrim, the *persona* who emerges at the very start of the *Tales*.

All of this appears very confusing. Why so many voices? Why do some appear more important than others? What is the precise role of each? Why do so many of them appear, disappear and, occasionally, appear again with baffling inconsistency? How are their voices to be identified in the first place? This chapter is an attempt to help you discover and explore these different voices, to discuss their roles and examine the effect such voices are likely to have upon the individual stories themselves.

The first extract is from the *Miller's Prologue*, which serves as an introduction to his tale. It occurs just after the Knight has told his story and as Harry Bailly invites further tales. What impression do you get of the characters involved in this interchange? What effect might their personalities and the issue of their disagreement have upon the subsequent tale?

The Millere, that for dronken was al pale,
So that unnethe upon his hors he sat,
He nolde avalen neither hood ne hat,
Ne abyde no man for his curteisie,
But in Pilates voys he gan to crie,
And swoor, "By armes, and by blood and / bones,
I kan a noble tale for the nones,
With which I wol now quite the Knyghtes / tale."
Oure Hooste saugh that he was dronke of ale,
And seyde, "Abyd, Robyn, my leeve brother;
Som bettre man shal telle us first another.
Abyd, and lat us werken thriftily."
  "By Goddes soule," quod he, "that wol / nat I;
For I wol speke or elles go my wey."
Oure Hoost answerde, "Tel on, a devel wey!
Thou art a fool; thy wit is overcome."
  "Now herkneth," quod the Millere, "alle and / some!
But first I make a protestacioun
That I am dronke; I knowe it by my soun.
And therfore if that I mysspeke or seye,
Wyte it the ale of Southwerk, I you preye.
For I wol telle a legende and a lyf
Bothe of a carpenter and of his wyf,
How that a clerk hath set the wrightes cappe."
  The Reve answerde and seyde, "Stynt thy / clappe!
Lat be thy lewed dronken harlotrye.
It is a synne and eek a greet folye
To apeyren any man, or hym defame,
And eek to bryngen wyves in swich fame.
Thou mayst ynogh of othere thynges seyn."

This dronke Millere spak ful soone ageyn
And seyde, "Leve brother Osewold,
Who hath no wyf, he is no cokewold.
But I sey nat therfore that thou art oon;

(I (A), ll.3120–53)

Here the teller of the *Miller's Tale* speaks for the first time. Our impression of him is both an immediate and forceful one for he is so drunk that he can hardly sit on his horse. He refuses to take off his hood and show courtesy towards anyone, particularly the Knight, teller of the previous tale and his social superior. He speaks 'in Pilates voys', loud and ranting, straight away peppering his speech with a string of oaths such as 'By armes, and by blood and/bones', and 'By Goddes soule'.

This coarse, foul-mouthed drunkard amusingly declares he will tell 'a noble tale', one that will match or even better the Knight's. Having quickly established through its portrayal of character the likely tenor of the tale to come (lewd and low!), this passage also draws our attention to something else, an external dramatic device or frame that might, at least in part, help to structure the collection of stories that comprises the *Tales*. What do you make of the Miller's reference to 'quiting' the *Knight's Tale*? It indicates the way in which tales are told in turn as part of a contest; it also simultaneously points towards ways in which they might be interrelated. Thus, in a few short lines, Chaucer establishes the drama of his work, indicates an ordering structure, and hints at a possible manner of reading the stories – in relation to speakers, and in relation to each other.

Does your closer reading confirm any of these ideas? The Miller's character is embellished by his belligerent insistence that he *will* speak as well as by his open, almost child-like admission 'that I am dronke; I knowe it by my soun'. Our immediate impression is that the Miller is frequently drunk and so knows only too well what he sounds like when he is. We are told that the Miller 'for dronken was al pale', that he was 'dronke/of ale', that he speaks 'dronken harlotrye', and that he is 'this dronke Millere'. The repetition of the key word, 'dronke' or 'dronken', reinforces our first impression, and emphasises the Miller's appalling behaviour.

He declares that he will tell of a carpenter and his wife, the former deceived by a clerk, and hints that his story is likely to be lewd with his warning that if 'I mysspeke or seye' it can be blamed on the Southwark ale. This comment whets our appetite for the tale to come, an idea compounded by the Host's attempts to prevent the Miller from speaking, as well as by the sudden and unexpected interruption of the Reeve who responds most aggressively to the Miller's plot outline, crying 'Stynt thy clappe!' and 'Lat be thy lewed dronken harlotrye'. The Reeve continues, warning that it is both sin and folly to 'apeyren' or slander a man or his wife.

Why this abrupt dismissal of the *Miller's Tale* before it has even begun? What is implied is that the Miller somehow intends to slight the Reeve, who is also a carpenter by trade, or at least that is how the Reeve interprets it. The drunken Miller's response is even more interesting. He makes no attempt to totally refute the suggestion but his reply does intimate that he is not entirely unaware of the Reeve's implication. He remarks that a man who has no wife cannot be cuckolded by her adulterous behaviour, adding 'But I sey nat therfore that thou art oon'.

On the surface he claims that he is not calling the Reeve a cuckold, but his remark is a sly hint about the Reeve's personal and private life, a knowledge presumably only shared by the assembled company of pilgrims who comprise the dramatic audience of the fictional story contest. At the same time he offers a clue about the likely outcome of his tale of a carpenter and his wife. Is his story about the Reeve or is it an opportunity to generally disparage him or his kind? What is clearly at work here is an interaction which can only be part of an external, dramatic device where one pilgrim feels himself to be the subject of a malicious or vindictive attack, but where the question of a tale's intent is also raised. We know that the Miller is planning to tell an uncouth ribald tale, one possibly designed to 'quite' the Reeve as well as the Knight. How then is it to be read in the light of the one that follows it, the Reeve's, as well as the one preceding it, the Knight's? You may care to read these tales for yourself. Also, does the Miller's behaviour here confirm what we already know of him from the *General Prologue*, and does he tell the tale you expect? Perhaps the most important question raised by this little exchange is one of interaction and juxtaposition of tales in terms of both style and content.

Finally the Host's role further enhances Chaucer's 'fixing' device of the dramatic frame. Here we see Harry in control of the proceedings, recognising that the Miller is 'dronke of ale' and immediately intervening to ask him to wait, to let another have a turn in the contest. You might already have noticed that Harry Bailly is a man quick to anger. His response to the Miller's insistence is to swear and impatiently declare 'Thou art a fool; thy wit is overcome'.

This extract enables us to identify several speakers or voices. Each speaks and behaves in a way that both characterises them and places them in a drama, a structuring device. What is also suggested is that individual stories might work in conjunction with or contrast to others, while individual speakers may have some bearing upon the types of tales they tell. With this in mind, read the next extract.

> I rede that oure Hoost heere shal bigynne,
> For he is moost envoluped in synne.
> Com forth, sire Hoost, and offre first anon,
> And thou shalt kisse the relikes everychon,
> Ye, for a grote! Unbokele anon thy purs."
>   "Nay, nay!" quod he, "thanne have I Cristes / curs!
> Lat be," quod he, "it shal nat be, so theech!
> Thou woldest make me kisse thyn olde breech,
> And swere it were a relyk of a seint,
> Though it were with thy fundement depeint!
> But, by the croys which that Seinte Eleyne fond,
> I wolde I hadde thy coillons in myn hond
> In stide of relikes or of seintuarie.
> Lat kutte hem of, I wol thee helpe hem carie;
> They shul be shryned in an hogges toord!"
>   This Pardoner answerde nat a word;
> So wrooth he was, no word ne wolde he seye.
>   "Now," quod oure Hoost, "I wol no lenger / pleye
> With thee, ne with noon oother angry man."
>
> (VI (C), ll.941–59)

This interchange occurs just after the Pardoner has told his tale.

He immediately invites his pilgrim audience to offer their money in exchange for salvation. Several questions spring to mind as he does. Why do you think Harry Bailly responds in such an extreme manner, departing from his role as Host and forcing the Knight to intervene in order to keep the peace? Is this interlude merely for dramatic effect or do you think Chaucer has an alternative intention?

The Pardoner straight away singles out the Host, trusting that Harry's capacity as unelected leader of the company and instigator of the storytelling contest will ensure his readiness to be the first to offer money. Yet the second line immediately detracts from what might have been a reasonable assumption. Here the Pardoner declares that Harry 'is moost envoluped in synne', a personal remark shocking in its audacity and scarcely softened by what we can only hope is a humorous intent. It may simply be an unfortunate and thoughtless comment. It acquires a sharpness, however, when the Pardoner's much earlier admission is taken into account, where he directly, and usually falsely, impugns a chosen victim as part of his technique for instilling guilt and shame into his audience (ll.411–22).

That the Pardoner is here deliberately exercising his skills by calling 'Com forth, sire Hoost, and offre first anon' is reinforced by the sweeping rhythm of the subsequent lines,

> 'And thou shalt kisse the relikes everychon,
> Ye, for a single grote! Unbokele anon thy purs',

in which he unashamedly demands money in a manner totally against the spirit of both the fellowship of the company and the contest itself. His words are final proof that he is a highly eloquent and persuasive speaker, but also draw specific attention to his role as pardoner, to his boastful admission that, though he preaches against avarice, he is himself guilty of the sin, someone whose sole intention is to extort money from what he terms his 'lewed' audience (ll.391–4). Yet here he is, calling upon the Host, and others, to pay for the penance he is sanctioned by the Church to dispense; the insult is obvious.

It is hardly surprising that Harry Bailly responds as he does, but the question of whether he reacts to a perceived personal slight (that he is especially sinful), or to the Pardoner's contemptuous dismissal of his fellows (ll.400–6) remains unclear. What do you think? I suspect the former. The Host's reply is a complete contrast to the Pardoner's effective rhetoric. Examine the language carefully. It is a fierce and flat refusal, one which indicates that the Pardoner is more likely to offer 'Cristes/curs!' than salvation, the line break underscoring the insult which is itself a response designed to match the Pardoner's own derogatory comment that the Host is enveloped in sin; here Harry implies that the Pardoner is unable to perform his job adequately. He reiterates his refusal in an aggressive uncompromising style with 'Lat be' and 'it shal nat be, so theech!' Harry's language is coarse, degrading and contemptuous, a foul-mouthed attack on what he perceives as the Pardoner's lack of masculinity. At the same time he asserts his own in a macho swaggering manner, reclaiming his role as leader, one undercut by the Pardoner's breathtakingly cheeky request.

In contrast to the Pardoner's verbal dexterity, the Host speaks brutally. His scathing dismissal of the Pardoner's use of relics as religious artefacts intended to swell the Church's (and his own) coffers is seen in the comment that such a man would have him kiss his old underpants 'with thy fundement depeint!', and swear it was the relic of a saint.

His contempt is compounded by his oath sworn upon another famous relic, the True Cross, that he only wishes he had the Pardoner's 'coillons in myn hond'. He urges 'Lat kutte hem of'. Harry offers to carry them for him enshrined in 'an hogges toord!' In obscene language he calls the Pardoner a liar and a fraud, casting doubt not only upon the Pardoner's tricks of the trade, his box of relics already admitted as fake, but upon his masculinity, even his humanity. The response is vehement and vitriolic, with the Host finally refusing to have anything to do with what he terms another angry man, a remark that intimates the Pardoner's silence is one of petulant anger.

The exact form of this quarrel has a certain inevitability about it. Harry attacks the Pardoner's only weak point, the one thing he has not been honest about; though he brags about his sexual conquests in the *General Prologue* (VI (C) l.453), we are told that he is most probably a 'geldyng or a mare' (I (A) l.691). It is the only response available to Harry after a self-confession that defends the Pardoner against moral attack. The Pardoner seems unable to resist asking his audience for money, a request that allows him to enjoy testing the limits of his eloquent bravado. If the Pardoner is compulsive in going too far, then Harry has only one line of attack open to him. Equally though, he may well be responding in kind to what he assumes is the joking spirit of the Pardoner's speech. Harry may simply be making a coarse jest, one that the Pardoner misinterprets when he takes offence. What do you think?

This highly dramatic interchange once again highlights the external frame of the *Tales*, the contest and its participants. Like the previous quarrel between the Miller and the Reeve, it is extremely entertaining. Harry's shocking response makes us, and the other pilgrims, laugh both at him and the Pardoner whose dazzling articulate display has finally been halted. Does it do more than this, however?

The Host's contemptuous tone matches the Pardoner's sneering dismissal of the stupidity of his audience. Harry may not know what prompts his anger, but he recognises the Pardoner's contempt even if he cannot identify its precise target. Is Chaucer calling attention to the Pardoner's role as agent of the Church? As a character the Pardoner is exceptionally skilled in gaining monetary reward. Chaucer is also fully aware that audience and Pardoner are bound in a complicity that depends on the latter's eloquence and the other's guilty, even stupid, passivity. The audience is easily fooled and perhaps the Pardoner's disillusionment with himself and his fellows is manifested in the way he is simply unable to resist the opportunity to try out his skills on an audience to whom he had already admitted his purpose in preaching and to whom he has outlined his methods. Grace seems entirely absent from this interchange, as it has been in the Pardoner's admission that his intent is solely financial. Harry's terminology is focused on the material, upon testicles and excrement. Is Chaucer using these voices to suggest that a reliance upon material things, like relics or even money, is unlikely to bring any kind of spiritual reward? It is a question worth bearing in mind for later chapters.

The following extract, taken from the *General Prologue*, introduces a different voice, one speaking directly in the first person, not quoted dialogue as in our previous passages. To whom does this voice belong do you think, and what impression do you get of his personality and his role?

Now have I toold you soothly, in a clause,
Th'estaat, th'array, the nombre, and eek the / cause
Why that assembled was this compaignye
In Southwerk at this gentil hostelrye
That highte the Tabard, faste by the Belle.
But now is tyme to yow for to telle
How that we baren us that ilke nyght,
Whan we were in that hostelrie alyght;
And after wol I telle of oure viage
And al the remenaunt of oure pilgrimage.
But first I pray yow, of youre curteisye,
That ye n'arrete it nat my vilenye,
Thogh that I pleynly speke in this mateere,
To telle yow hir wordes and hir cheere,
Ne thogh I speke wordes proprely.
For this ye knowen al so wel as I:
Whoso shal telle a tale after a man,
He moot reherce as ny as evere he kan
Everich a word, if it be in his charge,
Al speke he never so rudeliche and large,
Or ellis he moot telle his tale untrewe,
Or feyne thyng, or fynde wordes newe.
He may nat spare, althogh he were his brother;
He moot as wel seye o word as another.
Crist spak hymself ful brode in hooly writ,
And wel ye woot no vileynye is it.
Eek Plato seith, whoso kan hym rede,
The wordes moote be cosyn to the dede.
Also I prey yow to foryeve it me,
Al have I nat set folk in hir degree
Heere in this tale, as that they sholde stonde.
My wit is short, ye may wel understonde.

(I (A), ll.715–46)

The opening lines indicate that this is an observer, one who is relating the events and tales of an entire pilgrimage, one who has already briefly introduced us to 'Th'estaat, th'array, the nombre' of those assembled at Harry's inn, the Tabard, in Southwark. This is the voice of the anonymous pilgrim who opens the *Tales*, a narrator who controls the dramatic frame. At the moment it simply sounds like direct authorial intervention shaping the material. He says 'now is tyme to yow for to telle' how the company behave during their night at the tavern. He also promises that after 'wol I telle of oure viage', the rest of the pilgrims' journey. The tone is personal, almost intimate, speaking directly to the audience using phrases like 'to yow', 'To telle yow', 'to yow for to telle', as well as 'I prey yow' and 'ye may wel understonde'.

There seems to be a pause in the narrative of the *General Prologue* as a whole at this point. The speaker summarises what he has done so far, 'Now have I toold you', and prepares for events to come, for the pilgrimage itself, how 'we baren us that ilke nyght', and tells how the storytelling contest arises, thus enabling him to relate the tales heard here. This is a self-effacing character who begs 'of youre curteisye' that we do not assume that he speaks through rudeness or malice. Instead he insists 'I pleynly speke in this mateere', and will carefully record the words and behaviour of those gathered at the inn, as though he speaks their words himself. Here he assures us that he is an honest trustworthy narrator, an accurate one, one who takes his task seriously.

Yet he almost protests too much so that our suspicions are aroused at exactly the same time as we eagerly await his stories. The suspicion is that the content of some of these tales may well be salacious. The narrator's advance apologies for his material are intended to excuse him, but his insistence on a word for word recounting call attention to a wider issue, that of tale-telling itself. He reminds us that anyone repeating 'a tale after a man' must record every single word as closely as possible 'Or ellis he moot telle his tale untrewe', pretend things happened when they didn't or invent new words. He repeats that he is under an obligation as a storyteller to recount everything even if the original speaker is 'rudeliche'. The exact words must be recorded. In support of this obligation, and perhaps to alleviate some of his anxiety about his material, the speaker cites such exalted authorities as Christ and Plato, both of whom, he argues, advocated plain and direct speech.

Thus he apologises in advance for his material, presents himself as a humble fellow who may have got things wrong (he fears he may not have correctly described people according to their rank or 'degree'), yet is to be trusted to record events with accuracy. Is this the voice of Chaucer speaking directly to the audience? At the moment it might be difficult to tell though other extracts should crystallise your thoughts. If he is not Chaucer then why not and who is he? What is his function?

Here the narrator is seen as one of the company of pilgrims, one a little outside it, who records the details of this fictional journey, and is therefore presumably a character in the dramatic frame, another voice to add to the tale-tellers, and to the Host's. His is the voice that records and quotes others (notice the frequent use of 'quod he' in our other extracts), who describes them to us in the *General Prologue* and in the links between the tales.

At pains to denigrate his own authorial skill or role, his insistence on his way of telling stories calls attention to its inherent difficulties, to notions of tale-telling and the problems of writing. Are we to understand that these tales are totally new and original, or are they reworkings of ones previously heard or read? How closely must an author follow his source? If he chooses not to depart from it, to omit or embellish, as this voice declares, then how is a story to belong to its teller? This is the problem raised by this passage. It is simultaneously part of a dramatic frame, a fictional device, and an invitation to consider other perspectives. Chaucer's collection of individual stories in the *Tales* is a varied one as we have already seen, utilising lots of different styles and techniques even within the same story, and involving one, sometimes more voices in their retelling. Is he then likely to subscribe to the narrow view of writing proposed by the voice here, or rather, is this anonymous voice another device or mask, just one 'sound' amongst the multiplicity struggling to express their ideas, their opinions?

Before you can finally answer, it might be useful to explore all of the extracts in this part of the chapter. The next passage occurs at the end of the section in the *Miller's Prologue* where this so-far anonymous first person speaker apologises for the Miller's tale and tries to indicate that not all in the collection are like it.

> What sholde I moore seyn, but this / Millere
> He nolde his wordes for no man forbere,
> But tolde his cherles tale in his manere.
> M'athynketh that I shal reherce it heere.
> And therfore every gentil wight I preye,
> For Goddes love, demeth nat that I sey
> Of yvel entente, but that for I moot reherce
> Hir tales alle, be they bettre or werse,
> Or elles falsen som of my mateere.
> And thefore, whoso list it nat yheere,
> Turne over the leef and chese another tale;
> For he shal fynde ynowe, grete and smale,
> Of storial thyng that toucheth gentillesse,
> And eek moralitee and hoolynesse.
> Blameth nat me if that ye chese amys.
> The Millere is a cherl; ye knowe wel this.
> So was the Reve eek and othere mo,
> And harlotrie they tolden bothe two.
> Avyseth yow, and put me out of blame;
> And eek man shal nat maken ernest of game.
>
> (I (A), ll.3167–86)

Here the speaker sets about introducing the *Miller's Tale*. The earlier exchange between the Miller himself and the Reeve, prior to which the Host attempted to prevent the tale being told at all, confirms our early expectations of the dramatic frame. Harry Bailly tries to orchestrate the storytelling contest which is rapidly degenerating into a more personal competition between some members of the pilgrimage. The drunken Miller's sly and apparently disingenuous reply to the quarrelsome Reeve has already set the tone for his tale. Here the voice behind the frame confirms those expectations.

Once again his apology serves a multiple purpose. We assume that it is entirely genuine. The speaker appears shocked by the Miller's behaviour, his opening lines intimating that he has perhaps not recorded the encounter in full, despite his previous claims to be trustworthy and accurate. He remarks 'What sholde I moore seyn', suggesting that in any case the Miller's actions speak for themselves, and that this 'cherl' will undoubtedly tell 'his cherles tale' for no one can prevent him. The very terminology indicates that the speaker's own sensibilities have already been offended for the Miller will insist on repeating his story in 'his wordes', his plain and blunt speech softened for 'no man'. The first person narrator states that he regrets ('M'athynketh') the need to repeat or 'reherce' it, adding 'I preye,/For Goddes love' that no one believes he does so 'Of yvel entente'.

So great is his concern to excuse the Miller in advance, and to distance himself from the ribaldry we are about to hear, that his apology is repeated on several occasions. He begs that those not wishing to read or listen to it 'Turne over the leef and chese another tale' for there is plenty of a more elevating nature elsewhere. These apologies pile up towards the end of the extract as once again his tendency to over-protest makes us suspect this speaker. Bluntly he states 'Blameth nat me if that ye chese amys', immediately following with 'The Millere is a cherl; ye knowe wel this'. Here the short abrupt phrases, broken by the pause or caesura in the middle, emphasise the Miller's characterisation. Yet, simultaneously, the same line calls attention to another element.

This speaker insists upon distancing himself even while he excuses his material in advance. If we are to be warned about the Miller, then the Reeve too poses a similar danger and, in addition, 'othere mo'. Such tale-tellers speak of 'harlotrie'. He urges his audience to consider this, to 'Avyseth yow', and so 'put me out of blame'. Similarly he concludes, 'men shal nat maken ernest out of game'. Yet these very words underscore the lewd and lively nature of stories like the Miller's. The first person narrator's detailed insistence upon apologising simultaneously emphasises the content of these tales, serving as a kind of advertising trailer and whetting the appetite of his audience. Far from turning the page or choosing instead a tale of 'moralitee and hoolynesse', many are eager for the 'harlotrie' to come. Even his suggestion to beware of taking too seriously that which is only a joke, only a 'game', contains an implicit challenge to most readers' sense of humour.

Thus his series of apologies have the effect of dramatic tension, yet also distance him as an author or fictional voice. At the same time, the dramatic frame is further embedded for he suggests this is a contest where 'storial thyng' is varied, where the reader or listener will 'fynde ynowe, grete and smale', might discover 'harlotrie', 'gentillesse', and 'eek moralitee and hoolynesse'.

Finally, the speaker also confirms his own role as fictional first-person narrator seen in the previous extract. Here, as earlier, he declares

> 'I moot reherce
> Hir tales alle, be they bettre or worse
> Or elles falsen som of my mateere.'

Once again he insists that his authorial role depends upon his ability to record faithfully or recreate the tales he has himself heard, regardless of his own opinions concerning their content, and regardless of his own beliefs or sensibilities. This declaration inevitably addresses the question of authorship. Here, once again, the suggestion is that a writer is merely an accurate recorder of stories heard elsewhere and told by others, with the added implication that he (or she) has no effect upon what is transmitted. This speaker offers himself as scribe rather than author. Do you think that this perspective is a conclusive one? Is this how Chaucer himself would have viewed the process of writing in your opinion?

The next passage is a very short piece occurring just before this same character tells his first tale. In this brief exchange what do we learn of both the Host and the second person in this dialogue? What tone is struck and for what purpose do you think? The dialogue occurs just after the *Prioress's Tale* and just before that of *Sir Thopas*, one of the two stories told by the second speaker, the fictional narrator of the *Tales*. To what extent does the passage alter or reinforce your first impressions of this character?

> Whan seyd was al this miracle, every man
> As sobre was that wonder was to se,
> Til that oure Hoost japen tho bigan,
> And thanne at erst he looked upon me,

And seyde thus: "What man artow?" quod he;
"Thou lookest as thou woldest fynde an hare,
For evere upon the ground I se thee stare.

"Approche neer, and looke up murily.
Now ware yow, sires, and lat this man have / place!
He in the waast is shape as wel as I;
This were a popet in an arm t'enbrace
For any womman, smal and fair of face.
He semeth elvyssh by his contenaunce,
For unto no wight dooth he daliaunce.

"Sey now somwhat, syn oother folk han sayd;
Telle us a tale of myrthe, and that anon."
"Hooste," quod I, "ne beth nat yvele apayd,
For oother tale certes kan I noon,
But of a rym I lerned longe agoon."

(VII, ll.691–709)

The *Prioress's Tale* is received with sober admiration, a mood broken by the ever-watchful Host's jokes. Having initiated this contest he is determined to keep it moving, and so turns 'at erst', for the first time, to the voice identifying itself only as 'me', the speaker of our previous interludes.

Harry's question, 'What man artow?', calls attention to this shy figure, one who so far seems to have blended into the background, indeed has almost disappeared from the fragments linking the *Tales* until this very moment. At the same time his question is more than a humorous dramatic device for it forces the audience to observe him more closely too. In effect it repeats our own query: Whose is this voice and what kind of speaker is this?

The Host's description is a comic one emphasising the elusive and timid nature of a character whose eyes are firmly fixed on the ground in serious concentration, staring 'as thou woldest fynde an hare'. Harry coaxes him nearer to the others, urges him to 'looke up murily', and insists that others move aside to let him through. There is gentle teasing in the remark that his waist is as well shaped as the Host's own, a double-bluff for if this speaker is in any way a fictionalised Chaucer, then our surviving descriptions of the man indicate someone fairly expansive around the girth! He is termed 'a popet', a doll, that any woman might hold while his face is said to be slender and fair. Harry continues, claiming that he is abstracted, otherworldly, for 'He semeth elvyssh by his contenaunce'. The suggestion is reinforced by the comment that 'unto no wight dooth he daliaunce'.

Thus this speaker is depicted as shy, as one who shuns the company of others, is unnoticed and set apart from his fellows as perhaps befits the role of one who must observe and record. At the same time as it sketches in an important figure in the dramatic frame, one so far only identified by voice and not appearance, this abstracted and aloof air points towards a distancing which is crucial, and not solely in practical terms. It suggests that this speaker is not simply the observer and narrator of these fictional proceedings, standing on the edges of the crowd of pilgrims, but also that there is a distance between the depiction of this character and the author himself, that 'the murye wordes of the Hoost to Chaucer', the phrase opening the dialogue and naming this figure for the first time, conceals another ambiguity; the speaker both *is and is not* Chaucer-the-author.

There is a double meaning reinforced by the gently humorous tone of the extract. The Host tries to draw out this speaker urging him to join in the game, to 'Telle us a tale of myrthe'. This 'Chaucer' voice ('quod I') confirms the self-effacing characteristic of earlier, briefly pleading that no one be displeased, apologising for the fact that he knows only one tale 'lerned longe agoon'. Such an apology immediately reminds us of those previous ones. Is this claim to be believed? For the purposes of the dramatic frame, however, he is taken at his word and invited to tell what turns out to be the tale of *Sir Thopas*, a long and simplistic romance poem. This brief exchange is an important one. As we learned in the opening chapter, the character of this fictional voice might be revealed by details of his appearance and behaviour, while the interchange itself confirms our expectations of the dramatic frame. It seems to be a device to order and move on the different narratives, however inconsistently applied. It also lends dramatic interest or humour by introducing a range of voices or characters, and it confirms the Host's role as overseer of the fictional contest as well as displaying a more patient, gentle and urbane side to the personality previously encountered through our inevitably limited selection of extracts.

Yet the same dialogue also appears to contain an in-joke for its audience. The speaker is named as 'Chaucer' though his appearance pokes fun at the man himself. This Chaucer is an observer, and an author too but one so self-effacing he is almost invisible, and so unskilled that he knows only one simple rhyme. The joke is compounded when this turns out to be the dreadful *Sir Thopas*, a poem so excruciatingly awful that, as we shall see in the next extract, the Host is obliged to interrupt and cut it short. Is Chaucer (the real Chaucer, the author of the *Tales* itself) here mocking his own role as a writer? Perhaps the next passage will help you to decide.

The final extract in the first half of this chapter occurs immediately after this voice's tale of *Sir Thopas*, is, in fact, part of an interruption made by the Host. The narrative records 'Heere the Hoost stynteth Chaucer of his Tale of Thopas.' How does this 'fit' the dramatic frame? Who is the first-person speaker in this extract? Does it reveal any more about the craft of writing?

> "Namoore of this, for Goddes dignitee,"
> Quod oure Hooste, "for thou makest me
> So wery of thy verray lewednesse
> That, also wisly God my soule blesse,
> Myn eres aken of thy drasty speche.
> Now swich a rym the devel I biteche!
> This may wel be rym dogerel," quod he.
> "Why so?" quod I, "why wiltow lette me
> Moore of my tale than another man,
> Syn that it is the beste rym I kan?"
> "By God," quod he, "for pleynly, at a word,
> Thy drasty rymyng is nat worth a toord!
> Thou doost noght elles but despendest tyme.
> Sire, at o word, thou shalt no lenger ryme.
> Lat se wher thou kanst tellen aught in geeste,
> Or telle in prose somwhat, at the leeste,
> In which ther be som murthe or som doc-/tryne."

"Gladly," quod I, " by Goddes sweete pyne!
I wol yow telle a litel thyng in prose
That oghte liken yow, as I suppose,
Or elles, certes, ye been to daungerous.
It is a moral tale vertuous,
Al be it told somtyme in sondry wyse
Of sondry folk, as I shal yow devyse.
"As thus: ye woot that every Evaungelist
That telleth us the peyne of Jhesu Crist
Ne seith nat alle thyng as his felawe dooth;
But nathelees hir sentence is al sooth,
And alle acorden as in hire sentence,
Al be ther in hir tellyng difference.

(VII, ll.919–48)

The Host's interruption is blunt and forceful. He speaks plainly and impatiently, swearing by 'Goddes dignitee' and upon 'my soule'. He leaves no one in any doubt about his opinion of the first-person speaker's romance tale of *Thopas*, insisting that he is tired of listening to 'thy verray lewednesse' (stupidity) in choosing this 'rym dogerel' worthy only of committing to 'the devel'. In fact his ears are aching from this 'drasty speche', and he flatly refuses to allow him to continue in this vein.

When the speaker attempts to protest, his simple 'Why so?' suggests he is totally unaware of the effect his tale has had; after all it is the 'beste rym' he has to offer. He cannot understand why Harry will not allow him to finish his story as the others have done. The Host sweeps him aside with a curse, 'By God', and a coarse reiteration of the worthlessness of his tale: 'Thy drasty rymyng is nat worth a toord!' He insists that this tale is merely time-wasting and announces that the speaker 'shalt no lenger ryme'. Instead he is challenged to 'tellen aught' in what Harry perceives as the more laudable tradition of alliterative verse or 'geeste', or else something in prose. With almost childlike enthusiasm the speaker accepts saying that he will tell 'a litel thyng in prose' (highly entertaining in light of the extremely long tale he recounts), something that only the most difficult to please, or the most 'daungerous', might dislike.

At this point the humorous encounter alters in tone. Previously the Host revealed a down-to-earth impatience seen earlier in this section whilst his interruption, his comment on time-wasting, and the proffered opportunity to the speaker all remind us that he is both a character in the entertainment of the dramatic frame, like the speaker himself, and overseer of the storytelling contest, orchestrating its proceedings. At the same time there is a focus upon writing itself.

In the extract taken from the *Pardoner's Tale*, Harry gave us his opinion in no uncertain terms of the worth of the Pardoner and his insulting sermon. Here he feels free to comment on the first-person speaker's ability to tell his story, dismissing it as 'drasty' 'rym dogerel'. Here too the Host acts as judge offering his view of the content and form of the tales told. Yet his voice remains only one amongst many other possible responses (see *Further Reading*). Harry asks for a story containing 'som murthe or som doctryne'. The speaker responds with a promise of 'a moral tale vertuous' having already accidentally provided 'a tale of myrthe' as he was previously asked (l.706). At the end of the *General Prologue* Harry demanded 'Tales of best sentence and moost solaas –' (I (A) l.798). These comments indicate that stories should both entertain and instruct, that however merry or amusing there should always be a more serious or moral side to the content as the audience, or here the Host, demands.

Is Chaucer calling attention to the role of the writer? Have any of the tales you have read fallen into the category prescribed by Harry? The *Nun's Priest's Tale* apparently contains a simple moral as befits its fable style. Does Chaucer provide anything of more substance? What about the *Miller's Tale* which seems to have no moral at all as far as the surface narrative is concerned?

The first-person speaker talks of writing in this passage, of authorship, rather as we might expect Chaucer to do. He reminds us that each of the four Evangelists tells differently the story of Christ's life. Yet their 'sentence is al sooth', their essential meaning the same. His words point to a diversity reflected in the *Tales* itself, and hints that his forthcoming story might not be related in the manner others might expect or might have employed themselves. His focus is very firmly on the craft of writing, however. Though a character in the dramatic frame where his simplicity is amusing, he is also the fictional narrator of the *Tales*. Earlier he insisted on the importance of accurate detail and faithful recording of stories heard. Here he suggests that there are many different ways of telling the same story whilst once again disclaiming his own skill: 'it is the beste rym I kan.'

Does this confirm our suspicion that this pilgrim, though named as such, is not in fact Chaucer-the-author but an amusing fictional mask behind which Chaucer might draw attention to the problems of writing yet continue to remind us that *all* is a fiction, that stories are altered, edited or distorted by the fictional speakers whose own personalities might affect their telling, as well as by the first-person speaker who observes and records events and tales, and by the controlling influence of Chaucer himself who shapes everything as he wishes? Through the ingenuous and apparently naive voice of Chaucer-the-pilgrim, Chaucer is able to set contradictory opinions in revealing juxtaposition. This fictional voice pretends to offer us accurate observation but his remarks make us wary. (A telling example occurs in the *General Prologue* with the narrator's comments on the Monk's disagreement with the teachings of St Augustine.)

Thus, the dramatic frame is more than an entertaining device to structure the individual stories told; it allows many voices to speak, each with its own limitations, and so opens up issues and ideas that resist being channelled into one perspective. Here, Harry thinks the tale of *Sir Thopas* is rubbish while its teller thinks it is good, the best he can do. Others laugh at it. Which, if any, is the 'correct' opinion?

Conclusion

This section has drawn attention to a range of characters and their interaction, and to the variety of voices comprising the dramatic framework of the *Tales*. We have seen too something of the function of these voices, their multiplicity of perspectives in general, and also their individual roles. In particular the Host coordinates and apparently judges the stories in the contest he has devised, while the first-person voice (often known as Chaucer-the-pilgrim) observes and narrates. Both invite our reflection on the reception of the tales (the Host) and upon the purpose and difficulties of writing itself (Chaucer-the-pilgrim). This has been revealed in a variety of ways such as:

1. close attention to language and word choice
2. contrast and juxtaposition
3. the context of the tales or the speaker's words
4. the use of dialogue, much of it comic, seen via differing styles (reported or 'quod'/ first-person/ term of address such as 'yow' or 'thou') and interaction.

Further Reading

There are several different ideas arising from our exploration of voice and narrative.

If your interest is in the dramatic frame and the interaction of its characters read the *Reeve's Prologue*, the quarrel between the Summoner and the Friar at the beginning of the *Wife's Prologue*, continued at the end of her tale, or the interaction between the Knight and the Host concerning the reception of the *Monk's Tale*. Similarly the Host's control over events is witnessed at the end of the *General Prologue*, in the introduction to the *Man of Law's Tale*, or his invitations to the Clerk, the Squire, the Pardoner, the Prioress and Chaucer-the-pilgrim where he encourages them to speak.

The role of Chaucer-the-pilgrim is another important strand though his appearance in the *Tales* is fairly rare. Why do you think this is? Read the opening to the *General Prologue* or the end of the *Miller's Prologue* to help you make up your mind.

The Host's comments on the tales heard are frequent. In particular read his comments on the *Clerk's Tale*, set against the Merchant's opinion of the same story, or his remarks concerning the *Merchant's Tale*.

Finally, whose is the voice of the *Retraccions* at the end of the *Tales*? Why is the dramatic frame not consistent? (See the link between the *Man of Law's* and the *Wife's Tale*.)

II: TALES AND THEIR TELLERS – THE *PARDONER'S PROLOGUE*, THE *WIFE OF BATH'S PROLOGUE* AND *TALE*, THE *NUN'S PRIEST'S TALE* AND THE *MILLER'S TALE*

One way of reading *The Canterbury Tales* is as a series of stories recorded by a fictional first-person narrator who observes his fellow pilgrims and listens to a contest judged by the character of the Host. What, though, are we to make of the presence of other fictional speakers? What effect do *these* tellers have upon the tales they apparently relate? Those of you familiar with the dramatic monologues of Robert Browning may have already noticed that some speakers influence the narration of their tales in particular ways, but, as ever, the answer may not be quite so simple.

Earlier we began to consider the extent to which certain tales 'fit' the characters of their speakers. As you look at the next extract you should reconsider this question. What the Pardoner says here is closely related to the tale he subsequently tells. What is the effect of reading his story *in conjunction with* this extract?

> "By this gaude have I wonne, yeer by yeer,
> An hundred mark sith I was pardoner.
> I stonde lyk a clerk in my pulpet,
> And whan the lewed peple is doun yset,
> I preche so as ye han herd bifoore
> And telle an hundred false japes moore.
> Thanne peyne I me to strecche forth the nekke,
> And est and west upon the peple I bekke,
> As dooth a dowve sittynge on a berne.
> Myn handes and my tonge goon so yerne
> That it is joye to se my bisynesse.
> Of avarice and of swich cursednesse
> Is al my prechyng, for to make hem free
> To yeven hir pens, and namely unto me.
> For myn entente is nat but for to wynne,
> And nothyng for correccioun of synne.
> I rekke nevere, whan that they been beryed,
> Though that hir soules goon a-blakeberyed!
> For certes, many a predicacioun
> Comth ofte tyme of yvel entencioun;

Som for plesance of folk and flaterye,
To been avaunced by ypocrisie,
And som for veyne glorie, and som for hate.
For whan I dar noon oother weyes debate,
Thanne wol I stynge hym with my tonge smerte
In prechyng, so that he shal nat asterte
To been defamed falsly, if that he
Hath trespased to my bretheren or to me.
For though I telle noght his propre name,
Men shal wel knowe that it is the same,
By signes, and by othere circumstances.
Thus quyte I folk that doon us displesances;
Thus spitte I out my venym under hewe
Of hoolynesse, to semen hooly and trewe.
"But shortly myn entente I wol devyse:
I preche of no thyng but for coveityse.
Therfore my theme is yet, and evere was,
Radix malorum est Cupiditas.
Thus kan I preche agayn that same vice
Which that I use, and that is avarice.

(VI (C), ll.389–428)

The Pardoner has just revealed how he delivers his speeches to the ordinary folk that flock to hear him. Read his opening comments again, paying careful attention to the rhythm of his speech which works to sweep us on with the power of his eloquence. This extract begins in a similar way. The Pardoner seems fully aware as a speaker that we have already been so mesmerised by his oratory that we almost miss the simple and frank statement that by this 'gaude' or trick he has earned, year after year, 'An hundred mark'. He himself reveals to us the clever tricks of his speech. The Pardoner tells how he stands in the pulpit waiting until his audience has settled before preaching 'so as ye han herd bifoore', stretching out his neck, surveying his audience like a dove sitting on a barn, a symbol that simultaneously suggests spirituality (the dove) and the prosaic purpose for which it is used, to gain money. He gives us the precise image of his head nodding up and down as 'est and west' he takes in his listeners. The rhythm of the lines carry us forward once again with their repetition of 'yeer by yeer', the internal rhyme of 'est' and 'west', and the repetition of 'and' which links his ideas. So captivated are we by this performance that we almost forget the truthful comment which opens this extract. In the same way we are shocked by his contemptuous reference to 'the lewed peple', the audience that he cons, and almost miss the fact that we too belong to this audience. The Pardoner has set out to fool everyone.

This speaker, like the Wife, is unable to get on with his story without revealing his character to us. Why do you think this is? Does it have any bearing upon his story or its themes? His personality is not disclosed by the technique of concentrating upon clothing, habits or personal appearance, the list of observable things noted by Chaucer-the-pilgrim in the opening chapter of this book. Instead, like the Wife's, the tone is one of personal confession.

We can only gasp at the Pardoner's boast that his hands and tongue are so slick and skilful 'That it is joye to se my bisynesse', not solely because it is true but because we don't expect him to be so frank. In fact this remark is the point at which the tone of the passage subtly alters. What happens is that he becomes more daring, more open, as he bluntly reiterates the aim of his preaching, standing here in the pulpit, addressing his audience of fellow pilgrims and mocking those, who like his listeners of the moment, are implicated in the pardoning process. The Wife of Bath's tongue appears to run away with her in a list of ideas and clauses linked only by the repetition of 'and'. In contrast, the Pardoner seems in total control. Look at the carefully contained and complete sentences. Do they suggest to you a man carried away by his own eloquence?

As the Pardoner reminds us that he preaches against the sin of avarice, the paradox becomes clear; he volunteers the information that this is not in order to correct sin but so that his audience will give their pennies to him, for 'myn entente is nat but for to wynne'. For a moment he breaks off to contemptuously dismiss his listeners once again with the shocking admission that he has no interest in redemption, only in his own pockets. His exclamation underscores this when he confesses that their souls can 'goon a-blakeberyed!' for all he cares. Not content with this, the Pardoner indicates that most sermons have an ulterior motive where personal gain seems to be the watchword. Some are designed to satisfy the speaker's own glory or to gain revenge, to flatter, or to prosper; all are hypocritical.

What is revealed here is not simply a declaration of his own and other pardoners' methods, but this character's psychological make-up, one which requires him to confess. Undoubtedly this adds to the drama of the *Tales* and to the interest of his subsequent story as the reader is alerted to the tricks of the trade he has previously outlined. Is there something more at work? Is Chaucer using this figure to suggest that the very men expected to offer salvation are themselves ungodly and flawed, that the process of pardoning is itself purely mercenary and not spiritual? Is he also demanding that medieval audiences question their own role in the pardoning process especially in the light of this fictional Pardoner's depiction of his methods?

He even has the nerve to announce that if all other methods fail he is fully prepared to single out individuals and publicly (and falsely) slander that person, who, though never named, is left in no doubt about his or her identity. In this way too he gains revenge on anyone daring enough to criticise his profession. The Pardoner openly admits his hypocrisy. He reveals that his 'hoolynesse' is a guise under which he preaches of avarice, though he himself 'be gilty in that synne', and which he apparently uses to lead others to repentance. He admits that he spits out 'venym'. This image of the poisonous snake is in direct contrast to the fake innocence of his depiction of himself as a dove, noted in the first half of this extract. It is a detail that alerts us to his hypocrisy and compounds his audacity. Finally he again repeats that his real objective is money, twice telling us that he preaches only against 'coveityse', and that the theme of his sermons is always that money is the root of all evil.

Thus this powerful voice moves from an almost casual declaration of greed and contempt for others into a clear and controlled confession of depravity delivered in a highly eloquent and persuasive style that almost detracts from what he is saying. Three times he admits that he is motivated by the same sin against which he preaches; his frankness becomes part of his manipulation of his audience as we saw in an earlier chapter. The repetition of 'I', 'me', 'myn', and 'my' reveals this speaker as highly dramatic as well as indicating his ruthless and selfish disregard for others. It also marks him as extremely self-aware. He can tell us exactly what motivates him with unself-conscious ease; he knows why he does it and how he succeeds – because he is clever and his audience gullible. There may well be a note of despair in his words, an idea later discussed in the light of some critics' responses to this passage. Are you able to detect anything here?

What is significant is the extent to which this voice almost overshadows the story he tells. What sort of story is it? Is it the sermon he effectively promises and if so what are the features of this type of story? What effect does his confession have upon your reading of the tale? Can it be read as 'proof' of the skills he has outlined? Is it a focus upon avarice or upon something else? Might there be an alternative theme centred around the figure of Death and concerned with the idea of grace and salvation? If so, does this affect your earlier view of the Pardoner's personality?

Our second extract is taken from the *Wife of Bath's Prologue* just after she has detailed at great length the sort of misogynistic things commonly said about women, and the ways they might behave in response. This long digression advises other women how to manage their husbands, ideas continued here. How do her words relate to the tale she tells in your opinion?

> Lordynges, right thus, as ye have under-/stonde,
> Baar I stifly myne olde housbondes on honde
> That thus they seyden in hir dronkenesse;
> And al was fals, but that I took witnesse
> On Janekyn, and on my nece also.
> O Lord! The peyne I dide hem and the wo,
> Ful giltelees, by Goddes sweete pyne!
> For as an hors I koude byte and whyne.
> I koude pleyne, and yit was in the gilt,
> Or elles often tyme hadde I been spilt.
> Whoso that first to mille comth, first grynt;
> I pleyned first, so was oure werre ystynt.
> They were ful glade to excuse hem blyve
> Of thyng of which they nevere agilte hir lyve.
> Of wenches wolde I beren hem on honde,

Whan that for syk unnethes myghte they stonde.
  Yet tikled I his herte, for that he
Wende that I hadde of hym so greet chiertee!
I swoor that al my walkynge out by nyghte
Was for t'espye wenches that he dighte;
Under that colour hadde I many a myrthe.
For al swich wit is yeven us in oure byrthe;
Deceite, wepyng, spynnyng God have yive
To wommen kyndely, whil that they may lyve.
And thus of o thyng I avaunte me:
Atte ende I hadde the bettre in ech degree,
By sleighte, or force, or by som maner thyng,
As by continueel murmur or grucchyng.
Namely abedde hadden they meschaunce:
Ther wolde I chide and do hem no plesaunce;
I wolde no lenger in the bed abyde,
If that I felte his arm over my syde,
Til he had maad his raunson unto me;
Thanne wolde I suffre hym do his nycetee.
And therfore every man this tale I telle,
Wynne whoso may, for al is for to selle;
With empty hand men may none haukes lure.
For wynnyng wolde I al his lust endure,
And make me feyned appetit;
And yet in bacon hadde I nevere delit.
That made me that evere I wolde hem chide,
For thogh the pope hadde seten hem biside,
I wolde nat spare hem at hir owene bord,
For, by my trouthe, I quitte hem word for word.

(III (D), ll.379–422)

We gain a strong sense of her exuberant and forceful nature from what Alison tells us. The tone of the passage is direct and personal. We feel that she is talking directly to us or 'you' here. Once again a series of intimate details convey this sense of personal gossip despite the fact that she speaks publicly to her audience of 'Lordynges'. We are amused by the private wisdom she offers at the same time as we feel uncomfortable about its open admission. The style of the extract confirms everything we saw in our earlier discussions of the Wife.

Phrases like 'ye have under-stonde', 'al swich wit is yeven us in oure byrthe', and 'every man this tale I telle', are designed to include us in her conversation. The repetition of 'I' underscores the fact that these ideas are her own personal thoughts and add to the air of intimate revelation. Exclamations and conversational asides also contribute to the warm informal tone. She remarks,

> 'O lord! The peyne I dide hem and the wo,
> Ful giltelees, by Goddes sweete pyne!'

and

> 'Yet tikled I his herte, for that he
> Wende that I hadde of hym so greet chiertee!'

as well as offering other examples such as 'I swoor' and 'by my trouthe'. Alison's terminology is everyday. She speaks of 'wenches' or 'wenches that he dighte' (had sex with), of 'murmur or grucchyng' (grumbling and complaining), and her ability to 'chide'. Her speech is coloured by the frequent use of proverbial sayings or popular folk wisdom such as 'Whoso that first to mille comth, first grynt', 'With empty hand men may none haukes lure', and her comment on the aged bodies of her elderly spouses, 'in bacon hadde I nevere delit'.

The Wife's words are lively, amusing and engaging. Yet there is also a suggestion that this may well be the rambling of an old woman prattling away in the company of other females where such remarks are not to be taken seriously, and lack the weight of reasoned or well-known authorities. What is asserted here is personal experience, a knowledge gained first hand and passed on direct to others. Is this any more or less authoritative than other experience do you think? An ambiguity continues to surround Chaucer's portrait of the Wife. Does it help in any way to remember that this is a character drawn by a man? Is Chaucer sympathetic to the Wife and the problems she discusses or is she a stereotypical and threatening figure, a virago?

We gain such a strong sense of Alison's personality that her voice, like the Pardoner's, threatens to overshadow her tale. How are her remarks relevant to the story she relates? She tells how she tricks her husbands, swearing that in a drunken stupor they have repeated anti-feminist and destructive comments about women, and even calling upon others like 'my nece' as witness. These false accusations provide an opportunity to nag and scold, to wear them down in an effort to ensure she gets her own way in everything, and wins what she perceives as a war between the sexes. She declares 'I pleyned first, so was oure werre ystynt'. Fully expecting her men to attack her, for, she implies, this is how couples behave, she gets there first. Wearied by her complaints, her husbands are 'ful glade' to apologise for anything even though they remain innocent of the accusations Alison makes.

She argues that they have been chasing after other women though 'for syk' they could hardly stand, and insists that her own nocturnal exploits are for the sole purpose of checking on her 'rivals'. In bed too there is no escape for her men, for there she grumbles and complains, even pretending to refuse to stay with them if an arm creeps over to her side until 'he had maad his raunson unto me'. During the day there is equally no escape for 'evere I wolde hem chide', matching them word for word, and refusing to be a quiet and dutiful wife. She insists that had the Pope himself been present at their dinner table 'I wolde nat spare hem'.

In public and in private she acts out a drama. Her married life is based on a fiction where she pretends to be jealous and manipulates her husbands, all with one aim in mind. She pursues her own pleasures but marital sex is equated only with money or personal advantage. Is she perhaps accepting here a reality concerning medieval marriage and making the best of a bad job? Undoubtedly her portrait of the institution of marriage is a damning one; what is implied is that she is behaving exactly as men expect, as a gossip and a scold, a domestic tyrant, sexually voracious, or an untrustworthy free-spending monster. Does her amusing boastful bravado distance her from this reality and hide her own distress that it should be so? It is an issue worth thinking about, and one to which we shall return in Part 2 of this book.

Like the Pardoner, Alison is able to tell us exactly what she does and, in part, why she does it. She seems amazed by the irony that she only gets away with this behaviour because she plays her part so well that 'tikled I his herte'. Her sexual demands and jealous accusations convince her husbands that she has 'greet chiertee!' or affection for them. In truth, it is a 'colour', a deception enabling her to conduct her own affairs and have 'myrthe' or fun. She says 'I suffre' the sexual performances of her husbands, and admits that her 'appetit' is 'feyned' for she had no pleasure, or 'delit', in their aged bodies. She passes on her wisdom that 'al is for to selle'; she endures married sex only for profit, remarking 'For wynnyng wolde I al his lust endure'. At the same time she uses her self-declared and natural talent for deception and tall-tale telling, one applicable to all women or so she says, to ensure 'I hadde the bettre in ech degree'. Is this the crux of her confession, that she behaves exactly as men expect her to behave in order to gain 'maistrie', the upper hand, to win the 'werre'?

Alison tells a fairy story in which the 'lothly' lady behaves in a charming and courteous manner towards her chosen knight, but nevertheless deceives him into thinking she is an ugly old hag. Her true youthful and lovely nature is revealed only when he passes her test and agrees to surrender 'maistrie', a gift which she ultimately returns to him. Does the Wife use this story to express something of her own desires? Or, is she also, as a fictional voice, a vehicle for Chaucer's discussion of male and female relationships, already highlighted in her *Prologue* as we have just seen? Such questions may well have a bearing upon your reading of the next extract.

The day was come that homward moste he / tourne.
And in his wey it happed hym to ryde,
In al this care, under a forest syde,
Wher as he saugh upon a daunce go
Of ladyes foure and twenty, and yet mo;
Toward the whiche daunce he drow ful yerne,
In hope that som wysdom sholde he lerne.
But certeinly, er he cam fully there,
Vanysshed was this daunce, he nyste where.
No creature saugh he that bar lyf,
Save on the grene he saugh sittynge a wyf –
A fouler wight ther may no man devyse.
Agayn the knyght this olde wyf gan ryse,

And seyde, "Sire knyght, heer forth ne lith no / wey.
Tel me what that ye seken, by youre fey!
Paraventure it may the bettre be;
Thise olde folk kan muchel thyng," quod she.
"My leeve mooder," quod this knyght, "cer-/teyn
I nam but deed but if that I kan seyn
What thyng it is that wommen moost desire.
Koude ye me wisse, I wolde wel quite youre hire."
"Plight me thy trouthe heere in myn hand," / quod she,
"The nexte thyng that I requere thee,
Thou shalt it do, if it lye in thy myght,
And I wol telle it yow er it be nyght."
"Have heer my trouthe," quod the knyght, / "I grante."
"Thanne," quod she, "I dar me wel avante
Thy lyf is sauf, for I wol stonde therby
Upon my lyf, the queene wol seye as I.

(III (D), ll.988–1016)

What sort of story is this? Its opening places it in 'th'olde dayes', in a time long past when fairies filled the land and knights were bound by notions of feudal honour. One knight, under pain of death for raping a young lady, is set the task of discovering what it is that women most desire. He is given a year and a day in which to do this. Immediately what springs to mind is a fairy story where the protagonist receives the near-impossible task of discovering some secret or solving a riddle.

Several textual details confirm this reading. Almost nearing the end of his quest the lone knight turns for home in despair. By chance he rides close to the margins of the forest. There he is drawn to the sight of many ladies dancing. He approaches 'In hope that som wysdom sholde he lerne', but before he can reach them they disappear, 'he nyste where'. Only one 'creature' remains, an ancient old crone 'fouler' than anyone could imagine. She is a fairy-tale figure, a possessor of knowledge, who reminds him that 'Thise olde folk kan muchel thyng'. She speaks as though she has been expecting him and demands to know what he is seeking. The knight tells her, promising to reward her if she can give him the answer. In return he must 'Plight me thy trouthe' and now finds that he has entered into yet another agreement vowing to do the very next thing she demands, a favour she will ask 'er it be nyght'.

These details, the supernatural forest clearing, the magical time scale, the disappearing dancing women, the old crone, the promises extracted in return for information, all mark this as a fairy story. Its language and its constructions also confirm that belief. The dialogue between the errant knight and the old lady is highly stylized and formal, and hinges upon the pledging of honour. It uses words such as 'Plight', 'trouthe', 'grante', and phrases like 'Sire knyght' and 'My leeve mooder'. The passage's rhythm is slow and dreamy. Look at the opening lines of the tale, the start of this passage, or at the following section:

> But certeinly, er he cam fully there,
> Vanysshed was this daunce, he nyght where.
> No creature saugh he that bar lyf,
> Save on the grene he saugh sittynge a wyf –
> A fouler wight ther may no man devyse.

All contribute to an air of unreality.

Establishing the genre of the tale is fairly easy, but how do these features relate to the *Wife's Prologue*? The knight's riddle focuses very firmly upon the struggle between the sexes, the 'werre' of the previous extract where it is suggested that women are required to manipulate men in order to achieve their desires, and where neither sex seems to have any real understanding of the other. The knight approaches the joyful band of women engaged in 'a daunce' (the 'old daunce' or sexual dalliance which Alison nostalgically recalls in her *Prologue*?) 'som wysdom' to learn. The dancers vanish into thin air. Is the suggestion that women have some mystery or knowledge kept secret from men, an awareness of their own sexuality perhaps or simply personal experiential knowledge, an 'experience' opposed to masculine 'auctoritee'? The old crone promises to reveal something so powerful that it will save the knight's life and extracts from him a promise. The knight's response is to first notice her age and lack of beauty, an indication perhaps that men prize youth and loveliness above all else. The *Wife's Prologue* might be said to open up the question of what men and women want or need from each other. Her tale is *one* answer to that question. Look at its ending. Are we meant to take it seriously, do you think? How and why does the Wife's voice reassert itself?

Why choose a fairy story at all? Is Chaucer indicating that the *Wife's Tale* with its idealised ending is a reflection of Alison's own final love match with Jankyn and her craving for affection? Is he calling into question her interpretation of that marriage, intimating that it is more wishful thinking than fact? Is Chaucer also pointing towards the near impossibility of mutual love and respect between the sexes in medieval society by opening up discussion of the issue in this form? As usual there are no definitive answers to the problems raised by this poem.

Other tales take very different forms. Both the Wife and the Pardoner tell stories that are in some ways related to the tellers while their chosen genre (fairy tale and sermon respectively) has an additional resonance of its own as we have seen. Read the following extract and see if you can identify its form.

> Now, goode men, I prey yow herkneth alle:
> Lo, how Fortune turneth sodeynly
> The hope and pryde eek of hir enemy!
> This cok, that lay upon the foxes bak,
> In al his drede unto the fox he spak,
> And seyde, "Sire, if that I were as ye,
> Yet sholde I seyn, as wys God helpe me,
> 'Turneth agayn, ye proude cherles alle!
> A verray pestilence upon yow falle!
> Now I am come unto the wodes syde;
> Maugree youre heed, the cok shal heere abyde.
> I wol hym ete, in feith, and that anon!'"
> The fox answerde, "In feith, it shal be don."
> And as he spak that word, al sodeynly
> This cok brak from his mouth delyverly,
> And heighe upon a tree he fleigh anon.
> And whan the fox saugh that the cok was gon,
> "Allas!" quod he, "O Chauntecleer, allas!
> I have to yow," quod he, "ydoon trespas,
> In as muche as I maked yow aferd

When I yowe hente and broghte out of the yerd.
But, sire, I dide it in no wikke entente.
Com doun, and I shal telle yow what I mente;
I shal seye sooth to yow, God help me so!"
"Nay thanne," quod he, "I shrewe us bothe / two.
And first I shrewe myself, bothe blood and / bones,
If thou bigyle me ofter than ones.
Thou shalt namoore thurgh thy flaterye
Do me to synge and wynke with myn ye;
For he that wynketh, whan he sholde see,
Al wilfully, God lat him nevere thee!"
"Nay," quod the fox, "but God yeve hym / meschaunce,
That is so undiscreet of governaunce
That jangleth whan he sholde holde his pees."
Lo, swich it is for to be recchelees
And necligent, and truste on flaterye.
But ye that holden this tale a folye,
As of a fox, or of a cok and a hen,
Taketh the moralite, goode men.
For Seint Paul seith that al that writen is,
To oure doctrine it is ywrite, ywis;
Taketh the fruyt, and lat the chaf be stille.

(VII, ll.3402–43)

One of the most interesting aspects of this passage is the presence of the fictional narrator's voice which reminds us that this is a story within a story, a part of Chaucer's overall conception of the dramatic frame discussed earlier. The tale of Chauntecleer and the fox is told by the Nun's Priest and, in turn, related by the fictional Chaucer-the-pilgrim. What is the effect of this, do you think?

In the first instance, the fox and the cockerel converse with each other in highly eloquent terms. This detail alone is perhaps enough to identify the story as a fabulous tale, a beast fable, where the animals have human characteristics and symbolise human values. The closing lines of the passage make explicit a moral – as might be expected of a fable. Chauntecleer is carried in the fox's jaws to the edge of the wood and near certain death before the same eloquence and chatter that has been his downfall now comes to his aid in a chance to trick the fox. Using the same flattery by which he was originally duped, Chauntecleer appeals to the fox's ego and sense of triumph. He says that if 'I were as ye' he would proudly proclaim his achievement in defeating 'ye proude cherles alle!', and that he would curse and loudly announce his intention to eat the cock he has just captured.

This presence of mind has the desired effect for, as the fox opens his mouth to speak, Chauntecleer is able to 'brak' free and fly to the safety of a nearby tree. The fox's response is both immediate and clever. He apologises profusely, repeatedly crying 'allas!', afraid that he has frightened Chauntecleer by bringing him out of the yard, something he did 'in no wikke entente'. He swears upon God that he will speak 'sooth', and that he will truthfully explain what he meant if only the cockerel will 'Com doun.' This time his plan fails for Chauntecleer has learnt his lesson, and curses both of them for allowing themselves to be flattered and deceived. Such men deserve never to prosper, says Chauntecleer, the reference highlighting that this is a moral for men not animals. The fox agrees, cursing too those unable to control their tongues, those 'That jangleth whan he sholde holde his pees'.

The language of the encounter is courteous full of 'Sire' and 'O Chauntecleer, allas!' as each tries to persuade the other to fall for his trick. It suggests to us that the beasts represent humankind. The fox feigns sorrow that he had 'ydoon trespas' in frightening Chauntecleer while the cockerel uses exclamation to provoke the fox into action. Chauntecleer claims that *he* would have cried 'Turneth agayn, ye proude cherles alle!', and 'A verray pestilence upon yow falle!'

In the same way the narrator of the tale addresses his audience urging all to listen, and stirring interest as he outlines the twist to come:

> 'Lo, how Fortune turneth sodeynly
> The hope and pryde eek of hir enemy!'

It is a rhetorical trick he repeats at the end of the passage as he expounds the tale's lesson, already outlined by each of the beasts involved. He declares,

> 'Lo, swich it is for to be recchelees
> And necligent, and truste on flaterye'.

The final words belong to the Nun's Priest. He warns that those who perceive this tale as a mere frivolity, 'a folye' about a fox or a cock and a hen, should look beyond the surface narrative for its 'doctrine'. He repeats this, urging 'Taketh the moralite', and supports his instruction by reference to the authority of St Paul, insisting 'Taketh the fruyt, and lat the chaf be stille'.

Thus it is entirely clear to us that this story has a moral and is designed to both entertain and instruct, as the Host earlier requested. It is a moral fable told by a narrator who reminds us that we should be searching for its lesson as we listen or read. Once again this fictional narrator seems concerned with the art of writing, with ways of telling stories, as his final words remind us. He is allocated a simple entertaining fable as the vehicle for his lesson. He orchestrates audience response by heightening tension early on and highlighting its conclusion. Yet it remains a tale within a tale while the very words 'ye that holden this tale a folye' point to an alternative, more superficial reading than the one apparently intended by the speaker. It is a story that might be read on several different levels.

What is Chaucer up to here? Despite the Nun's Priest's insistence on the hidden meaning, the 'fruyt', rather than the surface humour of his narrative, the meaning of this story remains inconclusive. Is this what Chaucer intended, do you think, bearing in mind your previous reading and the ways of exploring tales discussed in the first two chapters? Did he wish to multiply perspective, and to suggest that there *are* alternatives by using the device of a fictional narrator who recounts a particular story that may or may not have some bearing upon that same character's personality? Perhaps your exploration of this tale's epilogue, where Harry Bailly offers *his* interpretation, may help you to make up your mind. By adopting fable form, with its 'required' final moral, Chaucer is able to open up the entire question of ways of telling stories and their purpose. As you consider the final extract in this section you may like to contemplate the resonance achieved by the adoption of a particular form or genre on this occasion.

Up stirte hire Alison and Nicholay
And criden "Out" and "Harrow" in the strete.
The neighebores, bothe smale and grete,
In ronnen for to gauren on this man,
That yet aswowne lay, bothe pale and wan,
For with the fal he brosten hadde his arm.
But stonde he moste unto his owene harm;
For whan he spak, he was anon bore doun
With hende Nicholas and Alisoun.
They tolden every man that he was wood;
He was agast so of Nowelis flood
Thurgh fantasie that of his vanytee
He hadde yboght hym knedyng tubbes thre,
And hadde hem hanged in the roof above;
And that he preyed hem, for Goddes love,
To sitten in the roof, *par compaignye.*
The folk gan laughen at his fantasye;
Into the roof they kiken and they cape,
And turned al his harm unto a jape.
For what so that this carpenter answerde,
It was for noght; no man his reson herde.
With othes grete he was so sworn adoun
That he was holde wood in al the toun;
For every clerk anonright heeld with oother.
They seyde, "The man is wood, my leeve / brother";
And every wight gan laughen at this stryf.
Thus swyved was this carpenteris wyf,
For al his kepyng and his jalousye,
And Absolon hath kist hir nether ye,
And Nicholas is scalded in the towte.
This tale is doon, and God save al the rowte!

(I (A), ll.3824–54)

The story that has just been told by the Miller is a 'cherles tale' according to Chaucer-the-pilgrim who earlier recorded his drunken behaviour and warned the reader to turn the page if seeking a

'storial thyng that toucheth gentillesse,
And eek moralitee and hoolynesse'. (I (A) l.3179)

The Miller's story is peopled by lowly, ordinary folk – a clerk, a student, a carpenter – and its plot hinges upon a sexual fling and some coarse practical joking, exactly as we were warned and exactly as we might have expected of the Miller himself.

His tale has moved on apace. Just as we had forgotten all about John's preparation for the flood, Nicholas's cry of 'Water!' to cool his scalded 'towte' is the signal for John to cut the rope attaching the boats to the rafters. At once Nicholas and Alison, not in the least mindful of their compromising situation, dash into the street to rouse the neighbours who run to 'gauren', to gape, upon poor John lying in a daze with his arm broken, and 'bothe pale and wan'. Staggering to his feet he tries to explain but his words are drowned by the voices of his 'hende' lodger (remember the cumulative effect of this word discussed in Chapter 2: the irony of this description of Nicholas reaches a climax here) and his own wife declaring that he is 'wood'. They insist that he was so terrified of an imaginary flood that he has hung three boats in the roof and begged them to sit with him while he waits for its appearance. This tall tale ensures that the 'folk gan laughen' and crowd upstairs to stare at his handiwork. No one listens to John's protests, a matter underscored in the text by the internal pause or line break. Everyone swears that he is mad, a story that sweeps the town and is repeated everywhere. Thus his 'stryf' becomes the object of mirth, and his 'harm' simply 'a jape'.

It is humour that has been emphasised throughout the story, and the tale's climax underscores this tone. Reference to laughter occurs several times in this passage alone even though John has been physically and 'morally' harmed. He has been duped, cuckolded and unwittingly turned into a comic spectacle; this is the price he pays for his gullible stupidity and his jealous love. Absolon is almost forgotten. He has only been the catalyst for John's downfall. As a story this clearly fits the category of 'game' or entertainment. Where, then, is its 'sentence'?

The closing lines contain a dismissive summary rather than a moral, one firmly focused on humour. Word choice remains coarse. Alison is no longer 'Alison' but 'this carpenteris wyf', not a person but a focus for the narrative's events. Despite her husband's jealous (and justified!) care of her she is 'swyved', the obscene word sweeping aside all nicety or sense of morality, let alone love.('swyved' was the medieval equivalent of our 'f-word' and not the more genteel translations of most editions.) In the same way Absolon is said to have 'kist her nether ye' while Nicholas is 'scalded in the towte'. The earlier emphasis on the physical remains.

We see that the Miller's abrupt final comment attempts to close down any possibility of protest or deeper consideration of the tale's content; it is 'doon' and the tone remains lighthearted with 'God save al the rowte!' Plot, language, characterisation, the cracking pace and humorous tone of this coarse and lively story of ordinary folk are all details combined in its fabliau style. It has fulfilled its promise. Is it a tale designed to 'quite' or mock the Reeve as our earlier extracts might indicate? Or is it a contrasting response to the *Knight's Tale* of aristocratic 'gentillesse' and courtly love? It slots into the dramatic frame with ease, but does the ending call attention to another intent?

The Miller's closing remarks firmly suggest that the only appropriate response to this story is to share the laughter of those fictional 'folk' who participate in the final fun at John's expense. Yet the carpenter has been an innocent, if gullible, victim of Nicholas's sly duplicity, and of a practical joke which might have had more serious consequences. Does John deserve this even if it is a tradition of the fabliau form that old men are punished for their 'unnaturalness' in marrying younger wives? At the same time Absolon's sadistic response to Nicholas is to brand him with a red hot iron. The details are cruel, and only Alison escapes scot-free. Is laughter appropriate in these circumstances or does Chaucer wish us to consider the events in a different way? Does the chosen genre of the tale with its harsh laughter and riotous behaviour, where expected modes of behaviour (established as *one* example in the *Knight's Tale*) are turned upside down, call attention to the very norms it seems to satirize?

Conclusion

Chapter 2 introduced a range of techniques and skills designed to help you explore Chaucer's work. Both this and the previous chapter have attempted to build upon these expanding the range and encouraging close attention to detail in an effort to look beyond the surface narrative. In this section we have focused upon three interconnected issues summarised below.

1. Further revelation of speaker identified by:
   - tone (usually informal, direct, personal)
   - word choice
   - rhythms and syntax
   - asides, comments, narratorial intervention
2. The types of stories told. It is possible to identify genre by examining
   - language and rhythms
   - word choice
   - characters
   - setting
   - plot and plot outcome
   - the ending (does it have a moral for instance?)
3. How the tale might relate to speaker, considered by:
   - comparing the content of the tale, its chosen form, and its details with the character revealed in the *Prologue* and/or in the dramatic frame.

What is abundantly clear to us by now is that much of Chaucer's work raises more questions than it answers, and that the air of ambiguity we first noticed in Chapter 2 pervades the entire *Tales* where each individual story or speaker is very different from the last. The poem is an open invitation to you to form your own considered opinion, as the next chapter should demonstrate.

Further Reading

There is a variety of types of stories in the *Tales*. Here we have identified several which you might wish to compare with others of the same genre. If your interest is in fabliaux then look at the *Shipman's*, the *Cook's*, the *Reeve's*, the *Summoner's* or the *Friar's Tale*. For other fables you might care to read the *Manciple's Tale* while the *Parson's* (and possibly the *Monk's*) might be described as sermons.

For further examples of the ways in which a tale 'matches' its teller, read the *Reeve's* or the *Franklin's Tale*. (Bear in mind though that not every story is directly related to its speaker.) Other tales with strong narrators are the *Canon Yeoman's*, the *Man of Law's*, and the *Clerk's*.

4

Themes, Tensions and Ambiguities

I: RELIGION AND SOCIAL STATUS – THE *PARDONER'S PROLOGUE* AND *TALE*, THE *NUN'S PRIEST'S TALE*, THE *WIFE OF BATH'S TALE* AND THE *MILLER'S TALE*

In many ways the previous chapters have raised more questions than answers. You have been able to identify a range of techniques common to Chaucer's writing and use them to explore his work, but one problem remains and that is the question of Chaucer's intent – his reasons for using some techniques and forms at the expense of others. Is there a pattern to his ideas, do you think, or an easily identifiable set of themes or concerns behind the multiple voices of the *Tales*? This chapter uses the same skills as before in an attempt to open up discussion of this issue. Its focus is upon 'why' rather than 'how'.

The first extract is taken from the *Pardoner's Prologue*. In fact we have already discussed part of it in the previous chapter, and so remain aware of the range of tricks and rhetorical skills this character likes to use. This time as you read it try to focus upon the search for a pattern of ideas. Look at word choice or the types of things upon which the speaker concentrates.

'Heere is a miteyn eek, that ye may se.
He that his hand wol putte in this mitayn,

He shal have multipliyng of his grayn,
Whan he hath sowen, be it whete or otes,
So that he offre pens, or elles grotes.
'Goode men and wommen, o thyng warne I / yow:
If any wight be in this chirche now
That hath doon synne horrible, that he
Dar nat, for shame, of it yshryven be,
Or any womman, be she yong or old,
That hath ymaked hir housbonde cokewold,
Swich folk shal have no power ne no grace
To offren to my relikes in this place.
And whoso fyndeth hym out of swich blame,
He wol come up and offre a Goddes name,
And I assoille him by the auctoritee
Which that by bulle ygraunted was to me.'
"By this gaude have I wonne, yeer by yeer,
An hundred mark sith I was pardoner .
I stonde lyk a clerk in my pulpet,
And whan the lewed peple is doun yset,
I preche so as ye han herd bifoore
And telle an hundred false japes moore.
Thanne peyne I me to strecche forth the nekke,
And est and west upon the peple I bekke,
As dooth a dowve sittynge on a berne.
Myne handes and my tonge goon so yerne
That it is joye to se my bisynesse.
Of avarice and of swich cursednesse
Is al my prechyng, for to make hem free
To yeven hir pens, and namely unto me.
For myn entente is nat but for to wynne,
And nothyng for correccioun of synne.
I rekke nevere, whan that they been beryed,
Though that hir soules goon a-blakeberyed!

(VI (C) ll.372–406)

The extract begins near the end of the Pardoner's speech telling how he tricks his audience and just as he moves on to explaining why he does so. He offers first of all a mitten 'that ye may se', material evidence designed to work as part of his appeal for money. These opening lines immediately exemplify the themes of this passage.

Not only can the audience see this mitten but they can actually put their hand in it; the person who does so will, it is claimed, receive an immediate benefit because their grain will multiply. The catch to this is tucked away in the final clause of the sentence which suggests that this reward is only gained if a person is prepared to 'sow' an alternative harvest, that is, to offer money in return. The structure of the sentence emphasises the way this is almost taken for granted with its casual 'So that he offre pens, or elles grotes'. The Pardoner trades on superstitious belief in this mitten, one of his vast and profitable array of tricks and relics. For a small payment he guarantees success, but more importantly achieves his aim, seen later in the extract, which is 'for to wynne'. What is suggested is that medieval religion is a materialistic one based on the exchange of money, an indication confirmed by the remainder of the passage.

Having aroused the interest of these 'lewed' people the Pardoner goes on to interrupt his display of relics with a warning designed to evoke a sense of guilt in his listeners. The content of this warning is vague, a catch-all. He remarks that if any person present 'hath doon synne horrible', committed some act so dreadful that it has so far remained secret, then that person will find that they are unable to make offerings to his box of tricks; in other words he suggests that they are denied all saving grace. The only example given is that of the woman of any age who commits adultery. Whatever the sin such a person 'shal have no power ne no grace' to receive the benefits the Pardoner offers for, as if by magic, he or she will be unable to give him money.

Because the Pardoner has divided his audience into those who have committed 'synne horrible', and those others who are 'out of swich blame', he can cleverly blackmail his audience. *Everyone* must 'come up and offre a Goddes name' so that he might 'assoille' or absolve that person, for those who do not will be presumed by their companions guilty of mortal sin. Here he makes explicit the religious aspect of his role. In addition he reminds us that this authority has been invested in him by the 'bulle ygraunted' by the Church itself. Thus his appeal to the superstitious materially based faith of his audience induces guilt, a feeling that can only be assuaged by the

Pardoner himself or, more precisely, by donating money to this authoritative agent of the medieval Church.

Similarly the Pardoner sets out to prick the conscience of his listeners. He adopts a stern and moralistic attitude, beginning with 'Goode men and wommen, o thyng warne I/yow'. This is an abrupt change of tone after his invitation to examine the mitten. His warning is designed to bring his audience up short at this point. Not content with this, the Pardoner then becomes faintly menacing as he moves from 'If any wight be' on to 'any womman', and then 'swich folk'. Those listening to him feel that this could mean *them*. He ends by sternly threatening those who 'Dar nat, for shame' come forward and 'yshryven be'. Without necessarily understanding the nature of the Pardoner's complaint against them (which is in any case deliberately unspecified), his listeners can only respond to a tone designed to invoke guilt and unease.

What follows is another sudden switch in tone with the Pardoner's blatant confession that his role is based upon this 'gaude', upon a trick solely intended to win money. Here he is intimate and frankly disarming. We do not expect this truthfulness but he admits that in his preaching he tells 'An hundred false japes moore', and even boasts that his eloquence is so effective 'That it is joye to se my bisynesse'. His contempt for his gullible audience is expressed in the reference to 'the lewed peple', while his description of himself stretching out his neck to survey them, weaving back and forth 'As doon a dowve sittynge on a berne' is an image we discussed in Part I of the previous chapter, where it was suggested that the spiritual symbol of the biblical dove is undercut by the extremely prosaic reference to a barn, plus the contrasting serpent image where he admits that his sermon is 'venym'.

What is abundantly clear in the Pardoner's declaration is that 'al my prechyng' has one single aim: to ensure that his audience 'yeven hir pens, and namely unto me'. The irony is that he preaches of avarice though guilty of the sin himself. It is a confession shocking in its audacious frankness, and a point underlined by the Pardoner's lengthy clarification as he insists

> 'For myn entent is nat but for to wynne

> And nothyng for correccioun of synne.'

The emphatic rhyme seals it together with his sweeping and dramatic exclamation

> 'I rekke nevere, whan that they been beryed
> Though that hir soules goon a-blakeberyed!'

Again his terminology is deliberately prosaic. The suggestion that souls might engage in the mundane task of blackberry-picking highlights both his contempt for the people he is meant to serve and, once more, equates the spiritual (souls) with the ordinary and the material (blackberries).

Several features have probably struck you by now. First, this extract contains an emphasis upon the everyday, upon concrete objects or material things such as the magic mitten, the Pardoner's 'relikes', and references to the barn, to growing wheat or oats, to blackberrying. Similarly money makes a frequent appearance with the Pardoner calling on people to 'offre a Goddes name', to 'offre pens, or elles grotes', to 'yeven hir pens', all so that he might continually receive an annual income of 'An hundred mark'. He preaches against 'avarice' in order 'to wynne'. That he is successful is entirely due to his own 'bisynesse' and quicksilver tongue, clearly demonstrated in the careful structure of his speech with its frequent shifts in tone. A crucial element of his success is also the fact that he is sanctioned by an exceptionally powerful institution, the Church, which gives him the 'auctoritee' to absolve sin and to preach 'lyk a clerk in my pulpet'.

What is largely absent from his speech, however, is exactly what might be expected, namely a reference to spiritual grace or salvation. On the rare occasion it is implied, by the dove or his comment on 'soules' or 'correccioun of synne', it is immediately undercut or directly negated. What do these details suggest to you?

They may indicate that Chaucer uses the Pardoner's voice with its self-declared avarice, his contempt for the very purpose he so skilfully serves, to draw attention to the role of the medieval Church and the type of faith witnessed here. He seems to imply that one way of looking at the religion of his time is to suggest that it is driven by a selfish need for gain and reward. The Pardoner, and the Church on whose behalf he acts, is motivated purely by financial greed. Yet ordinary people appear happy to pay anything in return for absolution of the most shameful sins. Faith mingles with superstitious belief, and is often dependent upon visual or concrete evidence. The Pardoner recognises this and gives his audiences what they want. Thus he offers the 'magic' mitten and shows himself aware of the practical necessities of life where his audiences are eager to use the power of faith or the might of God to guarantee a better harvest and so ward off the very real threat of starvation.

Do you think this portrayal of religion is an accurate one? Is Chaucer condemning a lack of spirituality or praising the Pardoner for his awareness of how things actually are? Is he suggesting that wider theological issues like grace or salvation have little practical relevance to ordinary people who fear the power of the Church but are more interested in day-to-day survival? Or is Chaucer's intent condemnatory as he attempts to offer up the role of the Church for critical examination, and opens up an area he explores elsewhere in some other tales? (See the *Further Reading* section.) That, of course, is for you to decide.

The next extract also focuses upon ideas concerning religion and is taken from the Pardoner's actual tale. As you read it, try to concentrate upon word choice and word patterns.

> "But, sires, to yow it is no curteisye
> To speken to an old man vileynye,
> But he trespasse in word or elles in dede.
> In Hooly Writ ye may yourself wel rede:
> 'Agayns an oold man, hoor upon his heed,
> Ye sholde arise;' wherfore I yeve yow reed,
> Ne dooth unto an oold man noon harm / now,
> Namoore than that ye wolde men did to yow
> In age, if that ye so longe abyde.
> And God be with yow, where ye go or ryde!
> I moot go thider, as I have to go."
> "Nay, olde cherl, by God, thou shalt nat so,"
> Seyde this oother hasardour anon;

"Thou partest nat so lightly, by Seint John!
Thou spak right now of thilke traytour Deeth.
That in this contree alle oure freendes sleeth.
Have heer my trouthe, as thou art his espye,
Telle where he is or thou shalt it abye,
By God and by the hooly sacrament!
For soothly thou art oon of his assent
To sleen us yonge folk, thou false theef!"
"Now, sires," quod he, "if that yow be so leef
To fynde Deeth, turne up this croked wey,
For in that grove I lafte hym, by my fey,
Under a tree, and there he wole abyde;
Noght for youre boost he wole him no thyng / hyde.
Se ye that ook? Right there ye shal hym / fynde.
God save yow, that boghte agayn mankynde,
And yow amende!" Thus seyde this olde man;
And everich of thise riotoures ran
Til he cam to that tree, and ther they founde
Of floryns fyne of gold ycoyned rounde
Wel ny an eighte busshels, as hem thoughte.
Ne lenger thanne after Deeth they soughte,
But ech of hem so glad was of that sighte,
For that the floryns been so faire and brighte,
That doun they sette hem by this precious / hoord.

(VI (C), ll.739–75)

Let us examine what happens in this passage. The extract succeeds the three rioters' pact as blood brothers to ignore all advice to the contrary and seek out and slay that false traitor called Death, the figure that has already killed thousands before them. During their search for him, they come across an old man to whose polite and careful behaviour they respond with swaggering incivility. The old man tells them that he is desperate in his search for someone with whom to exchange 'his youthe for myn age'. He too seeks Death but in order to leave this life, not kill the figure of the same name.

The passage opens with the old man's insistence that the young revellers' behaviour is discourteous. He suggests that there is nothing to be gained by it and reminds them that they should treat him as they themselves would expect to be treated in their old age. His reference to 'Hooly Writ' recalls Leviticus where the Lord commands that the young should rise as a mark of respect when 'ageyns' or next to an old man. He indicates that there is no need 'To speken to an old man vileynye', nor 'dooth unto an oold man noon harm'. His mild manner calls attention to the unnecessary and uncouth threats of the rioters; there is nothing commendable in an action where youthful vigour gangs up against a solitary and defenceless old man.

He then attempts to take his leave of the trio with an apparently cheery farewell, 'and God be with yow, where ye go or ryde!' Immediately one of the group prevents him from leaving on the grounds that since he has just mentioned Death he must be 'oon of his assent', in league with him as a spy. His threatening demand 'Telle where he is' elicits a calm and cooperative reply. The old man tells him exactly where to find Death whom, he claims, he recently left sitting under a tree and in full view of anyone. Accordingly the three dash off in the direction he has indicated and find not Death but a hoard of gold coins, a treasure trove, the sight of which ensures that 'Ne lenger thanne after Deeth they soughte'.

The idea of the narrative is a simple one. Three latter-day yobs chance upon an old man and in the midst of their loutish and disrespectful behaviour fail to recognise him as the figure they seek, namely Death. Instead they find their own deaths in the shape of a lust for gold so strong that it sweeps away all common sense and all notions of sworn brotherhood. Selfishness rules the day. It is this which forms the crux of the Pardoner's story, a tale told as an example against avarice exactly as he declared in his *Prologue*.

The clues to the old man's true identity are numerous. He is an immortal, doomed to wander the earth citing 'Hooly Writ' and proffering advice which he knows will be ignored. His initial farewell advocates that God be with the three wherever they go, a reply that takes on the tenor of an ominous warning. Its chilling portent, its intimation that they will be in dire need of such help, is reinforced by his casual and veiled remark that they ought to treat him as they themselves might expect to be treated in old age 'if that ye so longe abyde'. It is later reiterated in his declaration

'God save yow, that boghte agayn mankynde,

And yow amende!'

Similarly his detailed instructions concerning the precise location of Death serve as an unheeded warning. He tells them to 'turne up this croked wey', to look for the oak tree in the grove where he left his 'companion', adding

'Se ye that ook? Right there ye shal hym
fynde'.

Even his casual comment, that despite their boasts to kill him, Death will not be hiding, is ignored.

It is a meeting for which the three are ill-prepared. That they are entirely lacking in any kind of grace is apparent from their uncouth speech. Their language is abrupt and insulting with 'Nay, olde cherl, by God, thou shalt nat so' and 'thou false theef!' It is threatening too with 'Telle where he is or thou shalt it abye', and full of oaths like 'by God', 'by Seint John!', or 'By God and by the hooly sacrament!' Such blasphemy indicates the extent to which they disregard the notion of heavenly grace and salvation, even though the old man has drawn attention to it by his allusion to Christ's death which 'boghte agayn mankynde'. The possibility of salvation and redemption is there for the three, just as it exists for all of us, something to which the Pardoner alluded in his *Prologue* when he offered absolution in exchange for money. But the young men ignore it and pay the price.

What blinds them is, of course, the pile of treasure. Its description is a highly visual one, emphasising its immediate attraction and, by implication, pointing to its obverse, the moral blindness of the three. The old man indicates the right direction with 'Se ye that ook?' and they run until they 'cam to that tree'. Beneath it they discover 'floryns fyne of gold ycoyned rounde', looking as though they might weigh 'eighte busshels' at a guess. The phrase 'ech of hem so glad was of that sighte' rings with telling resonance, while the 'precious/ hoord' is described as 'so faire and brighte'. It is avarice which will be their undoing as each selfishly tries to gain the money for himself, an *exemplum* the Pardoner drives home in the remainder of his sermon-story.

Here, too, the fact of the Pardoner's own self-confessed avarice and trickery compounds the issue and makes the presentation of it doubly problematical. His intent is a selfish and a personal one. At the same time as he preaches against this sin, this agent of the Church has the authority, and the intention, to win money for both himself and the institution he serves by instilling in his audience a sense of guilt of which *he* is oblivious, and which can only be assuaged by the salvation of the Church's pardon. Thus Chaucer sets personal and materialistic gain against spiritual and religious grace. By permitting the flawed Pardoner to relate this tale, it is made to seem an unequal contest as the profound significance of this crucial medieval issue is strengthened and apparent criticism made of his era's spiritual or moral values.

The third extract in this chapter also indicates something about the Church and its ideals and practices, as well as focusing upon depictions of women, a theme to which we shall later return. It is taken from the opening of the *Nun's Priest's Tale*. As you read it you will find several things to consider. First, what does this portrait suggest to you as it stands? Secondly, is your view altered in any way at all by reading it in conjunction with the description of the Prioress in the *General Prologue*? What effect, if any, does the fact that the Nun's Priest is effectively a servant of the Prioress have upon your reading?

A povre wydwe, somdeel stape in age,
Was whilom dwellyng in a narwe cotage,
Biside a grove, stondynge in a dale.
This wydwye, of which I telle yow my tale,
Syn thilke day that she was last a wyf
In pacience ladde a ful symple lyf,
For litel was hir catel and hir rente.
By housbondrie of swich as God hire sente
She foond hirself and eek hir doghtren two.
Thre large sowes hadde she, and namo,
Three keen, and eek a sheep that highte Malle.
Ful sooty was hire bour and eek hir halle,
In which she eet ful many a sklendre meel.
Of poynaunt sauce hir neded never a deel.

No deyntee morsel passed thurgh hir throte;
Hir diete was accordant to hir cote.
Repleccioun ne made hire nevere sik;
Attempree diete was al hir phisik,
And exercise, and hertes suffisaunce.
The goute lette hire nothyng for to daunce,
N'apoplexie shente nat hir heed.
No wyn ne drank she, neither whit ne reed;
Hir bord was served moost with whit and / blak –
Milk and broun breed, in which she foond no / lak,
Seynd bacoun, and somtyme an ey or tweye,
For she was, as it were, a maner deye.

(VII, ll.2821–46)

The tale begins with the depiction of a 'povre wydwe' of advanced years in whose household Chauntecleer lives. The details of her dwelling and her lifestyle are carefully compiled, and accumulate to paint an idealised picture of a humble but praiseworthy woman.

She lives simply in a small cottage on 'hir cote' or small farm which provides for all her needs. She owns little, just three cows, three large sows, a sheep which she presumably has no intention of killing for she has given it a name, and, of course, Chauntecleer and his hens. This smallholding allows her and her two daughters to be self-sufficient with, the narrator implies, a little help from God. Her poverty is established in only the second word of the extract. The widow's meals are simple and plain; she eats 'many a sklendre meel' unadorned by 'poynaunt sauce' or 'deyntee morsel'. Together with gentle exercise, this moderate diet keeps her fit and well despite her years for we are told that 'The goute lette hire nothyng for to daunce' while 'N'apoplexie shente nat hir heed'. She does not drink wine and seems to exist on milk and brown bread, occasionally with bacon or an egg or two from the farmyard.

These details are presented to us through a series of negatives which conspire to suggest a life of denial and emphasise the humble simplicity of her existence. We are informed that 'Of poynaunt sauce hir neded never a deel', while 'No deyntee morsel passed thurgh hir throte'. Similarly overeating 'ne made hire nevere sik'. The Nun's Priest states 'No wyn ne drank she'. She possessed three sows 'and namo', while 'N'apoplexie shente nat hir heed' and gout 'lette hire nothyng for to daunce'. At the same time too, her plain living is conveyed through a lack of colour or reference to monochrome which also serves to highlight the vibrant colour of Chauntecleer, her cockerel, a contrast that emphasises her own humility. Thus she drinks 'neither whit ne reed' wine, drinks milk and eats only brown bread for

> 'Hir bord was served moost with whit and
> blak, –'

In addition 'Ful sooty was hire bour and eek hir halle'.

What then is the purpose of this presentation? On the one hand it acts as a reminder of the human world in a tale apparently devoted to the antics of a cockerel. Chauntecleer, Pertelote and the fox become more than mere beasts, taking on human characteristics and symbolising the follies of the human world. The lesson of Chauntecleer's vain stupidity, and the amusing sex war that takes place between him and his 'wife' Pertelote, is, of course, intended to be applicable to us. That it is an authorial device is emphasised by its genre – beast fable – and by the contrast between the widow's home and the farmyard, between her humility and Chauntecleer's striking and foolish conceit. At the same time, too, her poverty reminds us that she cannot afford to lose her magnificent cockerel.

Yet the presentation, as with most of Chaucer's work, is more subtle than this. In the previous extract we related the passage very firmly to its speaker, and placed it in a wider context rather than simply discussing it as a stand-alone text. This is a technique which we can also apply to this extract. The narrator of the tale, the clever Nun's Priest, accompanies his superior on the pilgrimage, the ill-educated Prioress, and it is her portrait in the *General Prologue* that reveals a further twist to his story.

Chaucer subtly depicts the Prioress as a lady in high Church office who, nevertheless, has pretensions to worldly glamour that severely restrict her religious capabilities. Unlike the Nun's Priest, she is a simplistic and sentimental character with little real humility or genuine charity, let alone any profound spirituality. Having found herself without a dowry, she has most likely been placed in a convent by her family – a cheaper alternative to marriage. Far from aspiring to be a nun, the Prioress appears to treat the convent as a kind of finishing school for ladies. Clearly Chaucer is here offering up for discussion what was a commonplace of medieval life.

In contrast, the old lady of the *Nun's Priest's Tale* conforms more closely to the medieval ideal of simple virtuous holiness for women. The structure of her description matches that of the Prioress in the *General Prologue*, especially the lines devoted to her diet. Where the old widow eats plain brown bread, the bread of the poor, the Prioress's dogs eat fine white 'wastel-breed', for example. What is missing from the picture of the Prioress is mention of holiness, a telling omission. Here, a poor widow, a marital state approved of by the Church and written authority in general, lives in near penury eating simply and plainly, and existing 'By housbondrie of swich as God hire sente'. In short, since the day she was widowed, this woman has lead 'a ful symple lyf', one highly commended for it has been conducted 'In pacience', the most admirable trait ascribed to anyone but especially women. It is a virtuous simplicity and humility not even witnessed in the lives of her farmyard animals, the courtly Chauntecleer and his paramour Pertelote.

Thus the Nun's Priest is able to use his tale as a form of revenge, to 'quite' his mistress, the Prioress, in whom these qualities are lacking. At the same time this ordinary, apparently irrelevant, description enables Chaucer to open up even further a consideration of the role of the Church and the place of faith or religious values in all walks of life. Those, unlike the Prioress or even the Pardoner, who ought to subscribe to Church precepts are sometimes the very ones in whom crucial attributes are missing, and who belie the expectations invested in their office. This extract is devoted to the absence of sensual or material pleasures, yet the Nun's Priest's technique of using negatives – 'not this... none of that...' – actually evokes those same pleasures. Is the implication that the Nun's Priest, like the Pardoner, intimately understands those very sins against which he preaches, an irony that both confirms the corruption of the Church and its officials and yet makes its agents highly effective preachers?

Reality and practice thus remain very different from the ideal. In a similar manner, this passage also reminds us that an idealised code of conduct demanded that medieval women remain as either virgins or, the next best thing, widows, and advocated a life of patient poverty and humility in order to aspire to God.

Yet, at the same time as this description of the widow is clearly indicating that she is to be admired, the details also border on the sentimental and so detract from the intention. She is a 'povre' widow, not simply without money but deserving of our pity. She is old and lives in a small house with few possessions. Her meals are 'sklendre' and plain. She never tastes any dainty morsels or sauces, or drinks any wine. Here then those same details that earlier commend her as humble and virtuous simultaneously paint a sentimental picture; she is a poor old lady with nothing to her name, trying to eke out a miserable existence. Read the portraits of Griselda and Custance in the *Clerk's* and the *Man of Law's Tales* respectively for another perspective on the subject of idealised holiness.

The next passage takes us away from religion and onto another topic. It is taken from the *Wife of Bath's Tale* and occurs on the wedding night of the 'lothly' lady and her knight when her age, ugliness and base-born lineage are offered by her husband as the reasons for his lack of sexual interest in her. The passage forms part of her lengthy reply. As you read it try to find patterns of words or images, or clusters of predominant ideas. What is the theme of this passage?

"But, for ye speken of swich gentillesse
As is descended out of old richesse,
That therfore sholden ye be gentil men,
Swich arrogance is nat worth a hen.
Looke who that is moost vertuous alway,
Pryvee and apert, and moost entendeth ay
To do the gentil dedes that he kan;
Taak hym for the grettest gentil man.
Crist wole we clayme of hym oure gentillesse,
Nat of oure eldres for hire old richesse.
For thogh they yeve us al hir heritage,
For which we clayme to been of heigh parage,
Yet may they nat biquethe for no thyng
To noon of us hir vertuous lyvyng,

That made hem gentil men ycalled be,
And bad us folwen hem in swich degree.
"Wel kan the wise poete of Florence,
That highte Dant, speken in this sentence.
Lo, in swich maner rym is Dantes tale:
'Ful selde up riseth by his branches smale
Prowesse of man, for God, of his goodnesse,
Wole that of hym we clayme oure gentil-/lesse';
For of oure eldres may we no thyng clayme
But temporel thyng, that man may hurte and / mayme.
"Eek every wight woot this as wel as I,
If gentillesse were planted natureelly
Unto a certeyn lynage doun the lyne,
Pryvee and apert thanne wolde they nevere / fyne
To doon of gentillesse the faire office;
They myghte do no vileynye or vice.
"Taak fyr and ber it in the derkeste hous
Bitwix this and the mount of Kaukasous,
And lat men shette the dores and go thenne;
Yet wole the fyr as faire lye and brenne
As twenty thousand men myghte it biholde;
His office natureel ay wol it holde,
Up peril of my lyf, til that it dye.
"Heere may ye se wel how that genterye
Is nat annexed to possessioun,
Sith folk ne doon hir operacioun
Alwey, as dooth the fyr, lo, in his kynde.
For, God it woot, men may wel often fynde
A lordes sone do shame and vileynye;
And he that wole han pris of his gentrye,
For he was boren of a gentil hous
And hadde his eldres noble and vertuous,
And nel hymselven do no gentil dedis
Ne folwen his gentil auncestre that deed is,
He nys nat gentil, be he duc or erl,
For vileyns synful dedes make a cherl.
For gentillesse nys but renomee
Of thyne auncestres, for hire heigh bountee,
Which is a strange thyng to thy persone.
Thy gentillesse cometh fro God allone.

Thanne comth oure verray gentillesse of grace;
It was no thyng biquethe us with oure place.

(III (D), ll.1109–64)

Just as we saw in the previous extract, a quick glance at the way words and phrases are assembled indicates to us the content or theme. The key terminology seems to be the frequent repetition of 'gentillesse' and 'gentil'. The passage opens with a reference to 'swich gentillesse' and 'gentil men'. It continues, speaking of 'gentil dedes', 'genterye', and 'gentrye', as well as a 'gentil hous' and 'gentil auncestre'. The word 'gentillesse' is used eight times in total, with three occurrences in the final six lines. Without doubt this points us in the direction of a crucial issue.

Also important are words like 'vertuous' as opposed to 'vice' or 'vileynye', while the phrase 'pryvee and apert' appears twice. Similarly repeated are the words 'richesse', 'eldres' and 'biquethe'. The theme is clearly 'gentillesse', or nobility, which seems to involve private and public behaviour as well as birthright gained from our 'eldres'. Twice the speaker refers to God as well as to nature, as seen in phrases like 'kynde', 'planted natureelly', or 'office natureel', and indicating a division between 'gentillesse' which is passed down the family line and that which arises naturally or is intrinsic or God-given. How is this argument developed in the passage?

First of all we need to examine the structure of our chosen extract and the outline of its ideas if the key terminology is to be of any relevance to us. The speaker initially chooses to focus on her husband's comment on her lineage rather than on her physical appearance. At once she reveals to us what she considers to be the most important concern. She suggests that the knight speaks of nobility in its more usually accepted and orthodox meaning, claiming that it is 'descended out of old richesse'. She claims that he, like most people, believe that 'gentillesse' is passed on through an accident of birth, and that name, status and rank make 'gentil men'.

At once the speaker dismisses this notion with her 'Swich arrogance is nat worth a hen'. The statement is abrupt, signifying her dismissal of orthodox ideas, while the prosaic reference to a 'hen' has the effect of bathos. First she speaks of 'gentillesse' and noblemen;

the everyday word ' hen' is a contrast emphasised by its harsh monosyllable. That noblemen might regard a hen as any worth at all seems unthinkable, and hence the speaker's contempt invests this ordinary word with the status of a curse.

Her attack is partly personal for her husband is a knight of King Arthur's court bound by allegiance and honour, a man of noble birth and position who has nevertheless abused this earlier by raping a young woman. His wife's opening remarks quietly but firmly destroy long-standing notions and ideals.

She continues, urging him to 'Looke' at whoever is the most virtuous, and at whoever 'entendeth ay' or strives 'To do the gentil dedes that he kan', at *all* times, in *all* circumstances both 'Pryvee and apert'. This, she argues, is the most noble, not the one whose elders, though virtuous themselves, passed on a legacy of wealth and status. Families might bequeath 'heigh parage' or noble lineage, but the reputation for 'vertuous lyvyng' remains theirs alone. The crux of her speech is that 'oure gentillesse' comes from Christ, for of 'Crist wole we clayme...our gentillesse,' and not 'of oure eldres'. It is to be found in careful, thoughtful and dutiful behaviour, in those who always 'do the gentil dedes that he kan'.

The speaker supports her view with reference to common knowledge where 'every wight woot this as wel as I', and also to written authority, to the Italian poet Dante. She suggests that parents are only able to leave earthly or 'temporel' things which their children might destroy, might 'hurte and/mayme'. They do not leave us 'hir vertuous lyvyng'. A quality like 'gentillesse' does not occur naturally in everyone, and it is not a commodity which can be inherited.

In contrast, if 'gentillesse' were planted naturally in a chosen family, as opposed to being dependent on birth or privilege, then such people might always behave dutifully and perform 'no vileynye or vice'. She compares this to the natural properties of fire which will behave in a consistent and known way wherever it occurs. To repeat, what her analogy implies is that 'gentillesse' *might* occur naturally for it comes from God and not family name, but that it is demonstrated through consistently good behaviour; it is not a quality that can be bestowed by an accident of birth.

The final section of her speech clarifies her argument. Gentility, according to this wife, has nothing to do with possession or wealth. People do not 'doon hir operacioun', do not always behave the same, unlike fire which is consistent according to its natural properties and the laws of 'kynde'. She suggests that simply because someone is born into a noble house and 'hadde his eldres noble and vertuous' that birthright and 'gentil auncestre' does not guarantee virtuous behaviour in its recipient, as the knight has proved. Being 'A lordes sone' does not automatically mean that poor behaviour is impossible. Instead 'He nys nat gentil, be he duc or erl'. Her conclusion is that 'vileyns synful dedes make a cherl'. Here she indicates that it is behaviour and not social class, 'heigh bountee', or the renown of 'thyne auncestres' that demonstrates 'gentillesse'. It 'was no thyng biquethe us with oure place', but is something to be earned, not bestowed on us.

The 'lothly' lady's view is a radical and disturbing one, and a challenge to the order represented by the knight himself. Her comments invert orthodox notions and permit Chaucer to open up a discussion that ultimately remains inconclusive. The issue itself is a crucial one yet its presentation, or rather that of the speaker, remains ambiguous.

In the first place, the speaker – a woman – speaks with an authority usually denied to her sex. There are none of the ramblings, side-issues, or intimate confessions that we found earlier with the Wife of Bath. Instead, the tone is reasonable and logical, and is free of exclamation or rhetorical devices. The sentence structure is a complex one, carefully balanced with a series of semi-colons and colons as she develops an authoritative and compelling argument. One obvious example is the following quotation but there are others for you to find. The speaker comments on Dante:

> Lo, in swich maner rym is Dantes tale:
> 'Ful selde up riseth by his branches smale
> Prowesse of man, for God, of his goodnesse,
> Wole that of hym we clayme oure gentil-/lesse';
> For of oure eldres may we no thyng clayme
> But temporel thyng...

Similarly the vocabulary is, apart from 'hen', not at all colloquial or conversational. Instead it is largely impersonal, employing lots of abstract nouns. Again examples are numerous and include such terms as 'goodnesse', 'gentillesse', 'renomee', and 'bountee'. Word choice and sentence structure thus make this woman's argument a powerful, authoritative and challenging one that we are meant to take seriously despite its contentious nature.

In the second place, though, these remain the views of a fictional female character in a fairy-tale whose context is distanced from time and reality. She speaks to a feudal knight from a bygone era, a knight whose allegiance is to the mythical court of King Arthur where honour and chivalry were said to predominate. Is she attempting to correct her errant husband and teach him his obligations, or do her words have a wider application? She herself is depicted as the possessor of wisdom. She imparts this by helping the knight in his initial quest, and then by speaking authoritatively in preparation for her final magical transformation into loveliness. She imparts her knowledge in private and thus escapes the possible censure reserved for the teller of the tale – the Wife of Bath herself – who has earlier pronounced and proclaimed in open audience. Is Chaucer simultaneously advocating her ideas and detracting from them by making this perspective a private female one delivered in a fairy-tale outside and beyond worldly boundaries? Your reading of the rest of the tale might help you to decide.

Why does Chaucer raise the question of 'gentillesse' at all? Possibly this was an issue on the minds of those in the 'new' urbanised or commercial world where status might have been gained through the acquisition of wealth or business interests, where notions of birthright were beginning to be dissolved, and an already outdated concept of feudal honour replaced by a more flexible web of allegiance and connection. Perhaps this tale should be read with the values presented in poems like the *Knight's Tale* and the *Franklin's* firmly in mind. Chaucer offers one perspective here but clearly there are many others.

The problem of ambiguity is prevalent throughout Chaucer's work as we have already seen. How and why does the poet deliberately overlay his stories in this way? One of the sources of ambiguity in the *Wife's Tale* lies in its context. How is ambiguity revealed in the next extract taken from the *Miller's Tale*? What insights do you gain about attitudes to women and social class from this passage?

> She was ful moore blisful on to see
> Than is the newe pere-jonette tree,
> And softer than the wolle is of a wether.
> And by hir girdel heeng a purs of lether,
> Tasseled with silk and perled with latoun.
> In al this world, to seken up and doun,
> There nys no man so wys that koude thenche
> So gay a popelote or swich a wenche.
> Ful brighter was the shynyng of hir hewe
> Than in the Tour the noble yforged newe.
> But of hir song, it was as loude and yerne
> As any swalwe sittynge on a berne.
> Therto she koude skippe and make game,
> As any kyde or calf folwynge his dame.
> Hir mouth was sweete as bragot or the meeth,
> Or hoord of apples leyd in hey or heeth.
> Wynsynge she was, as is a joly colt,
> Long as a mast, and upright as a bolt.
> A brooch she baar upon hir lowe coler,
> As brood as is the boos of a bokeler.
> Hir shoes were laced on hir legges hye.
> She was a prymerole, a piggesnye,
> For any lord to leggen in his bedde,
> Or yet for any good yeman to wedde.
>
> (I (A), ll.3247–70)

This short extract is taken from the section describing Alison. If you think back to earlier chapters you will already be prepared for a double reading here, a surface impression undercut by the use of more ambiguous or slippery terminology. At first glance Alison is associated with a lush natural beauty. We are told that she is lovelier than the early ripening pear tree and softer than the softest wool. She sings loud and 'yerne' or eagerly. She is playful and skittish or 'Wynsynge'. She is compared to a variety of young animals – a kid, a calf, 'a joly colt' – emphasising her fresh and naturally attractive demeanour. She is likened also to the light delicate swallow as well as to lovely flowers, 'a prymerole, a piggesnye'. Her breath is as sweet and fragrant as 'bragot or the meeth' or else like a 'hoord of apples leyd in hey or heeth'. Her build is tall and straight, 'Long as a mast, and upright as a bolt'. Our overall impression is of youth, vitality and a natural freshness.

At the same time Alison is prettily adorned and decorated to enhance her beauty. She wears a leather purse on her belt, as well as a large and broad shiny brooch. Her shoes are laced high up her legs to draw attention to one of her best features. In short she is a 'popelote', a little doll.

However, closer examination begins to suggest something very different. First of all she is associated not just with natural things but with everyday or mundane items. As she plays and skips like a young animal following 'his dame' or like a skittish colt, her youth and natural ease also hint at a lack of elegance. These are humble farmyard animals. In addition she is compared to the plain and ordinary primrose, a pear tree, her softness to the wool of a 'wether', and her breath to the sweetness of mead or 'bragot', a simple country drink; all firmly indicate her class. Alison is 'swich a wenche', an ordinary country girl, and most definitely not a lady. There would of course be nothing damning in this depiction if it corresponded to a suggestion that she was natural and unspoilt with few aspirations or pretensions, but, once again, other features subtly undercut this impression.

Perhaps the most telling reference, one immediately signalled to a medieval audience, is to the 'pere-jonette tree'. This has an alternative meaning, hinting at an open, even lascivious, sexuality just as her high-laced shoes and strategically placed purse dangling from the belt defining her waist draw attention to her physical attributes. At the same time, soft natural images – such as wool, leather, silk, a baby goat or a calf – are set against a certain bright hardness in Alison that undoubtedly prepares us for her eager cooperation with Nicholas. Her leather purse with its silk tassles is adorned with 'latoun', a brassy metal, while her brooch is compared to 'a bokeler', the raised centre of a shield. Possibly worst of all is the comment that her complexion is shining, and is brighter than 'in the Tour the noble yforged newe'. The image is of a hard, shiny new coin, an unnatural and jarring association designed to bring us up short. There is then a certain ambiguity about Alison's portrait where her fresh, natural loveliness is undercut by a harsher artificiality.

It is not only details and images that accumulate to give us this impression. A second technique, that of juxtaposition, also contributes to our feeling that there exists an underlying complexity or ambiguity where Alison is concerned. Many of the comments here appear out of sequence or disjointed. The extract begins with a general description of her beauty, followed by a reference to her clothing, and back to an assertion that no man could ever imagine a lovelier wench. This remark is immediately followed by the allusion to a new-minted coin, and then skips onto an apparently unconnected comment about 'hir song'. This is succeeded by a host of references to singing, her movement, her fragrant breath, her build, her brooch, shoes, and the concluding and juxtaposed pair of references that she reminds the speaker of a flower

> 'For any lord to leggen in his bedde,
> Or yet for any good yeman to wedde'.

The drunken Miller, teller of this tale, might well have related it in this almost rambling manner. He gives us a series of quick-fire impressions of her sensual beauty. These snapshots reinforce the impression that, to a casual observer at least, Alison is gorgeous, at the same time as the implied contrasts cry out for a closer reading. She is all of these things, however contradictory, and no single characteristic can adequately summarise her. Thus Chaucer makes this portrait an ambiguous one where the only certain thing is that she is of a low class, a crucial factor as the final lines indicate. Alison is a 'wenche', one sexually available and beautiful enough for 'any lord' to bed. The additional comment that she is also good enough for a yeoman to wed is almost an afterthought; what is revealed in this casual and sly comment is that she is not suitable as an aristocratic wife.

Is Chaucer's portrait of Alison to be taken at face value as a depiction of a lovely and lively young woman, vibrant and naturally sexually aware, joyous and unrestrained, wanting to make the most of her charms before they fade? Or is there a darker side, a suggestion that women are sexually threatening (the pear tree), that even their apparently natural beauty is achieved through artifice (her purse, a brooch, the coin), and aimed solely for the purpose of pleasure? At the same time as Chaucer fails to resolve the tension between these contrasting and widely prevalent attitudes towards women, he once again raises the question of social order. The implication here, unlike the passage we previously explored, is that it remains fixed. As a lower class 'cherl' Alison can only expect to marry within her own rank even if a lord decides to bed her. Rights and privileges appear to be denied to women like her. Is it significant that she is married to an old carpenter when she so obviously prefers the company of younger men like Nicholas? Here too Chaucer calls attention to the Church's prescribed ideal of virginity. Her fun with 'any lord' seems not to preclude her marriage to 'any good yeman', and possibly highlights that gap between ideal and practice which so interested Chaucer.

II: WOMEN AND MARRIAGE – THE *MERCHANT'S TALE*, THE *NUN'S PRIEST'S TALE* AND THE *WIFE OF BATH'S PROLOGUE*

What are we to make of recent feminist interpretations of Chaucer? Is he a 'friend' to women, one sympathetic to their plight? What light, if any, is shed by exploration of the next extract taken from the complex and fascinating *Merchant's Tale,* where another old man, January, chooses young May as his bride?

> The bryde was broght abedde as stille as stoon;
> And whan the bed was with the preest yblessed,
> Out of the chambre hath every wight hym / dressed,
> And Januarie hath faste in armes take
> His fresshe May, his paradys, his make.
> He lulleth hire; he kisseth hire ful ofte;
> With thikke brustles of his berd unsofte,
> Lyk to the skyn of houndfyssh, sharp as brere –

For he was shave al newe in his manere –
He rubbeth hire aboute hir tendre face,
And seyde thus, "Allas! I moot trespace
To yow, my spouse, and yow greetly offende
Er tyme come that I wil doun descende.
But nathelees, considereth this," quod he,
"Ther nys no werkman, whatsoevere he be,
That may bothe werke wel and hastily;
This wol be doon at leyser parfitly.
It is no fors how longe that we pleye;
In trewe wedlok coupled be we tweye,
And blessed be the yok that we been inne,
For in oure actes we mowe do no synne.
A man may do no synne with his wyf,
Ne hurte hymselven with his owene knyf,
For we han leve to pleye us by the lawe."
Thus laboureth he til that the day gan dawe;
And thanne he taketh a sop in fyn clarree,
And upright in his bed thanne sitteth he,
And after that he sang ful loude and cleere,
And kiste his wyf, and made wantown cheere.
He was al coltissh, ful of ragerye,
And ful of jargon as a flekked pye.
The slakke skyn aboute his nekke shaketh
Whil that he sang, so chaunteth he and craketh.
But God woot what that May thoughte in hir / herte,
Whan she hym saugh up sittynge in his sherte;
In his nyght-cappe, and with his nekke lene;
She preyseth nat his pleyyng worth a bene.

(IV (E), ll.1818–54)

The opening line of this passage sets the tone at once: 'The bryde was broght abedde as stille as stoon'. Immediately it instils a sense of chilled horror in the audience, a sense of impending doom. The simile implies that May's cold passivity conceals her own fears, and even intimates that the wedding chamber is tantamount to a tomb. There is nothing unusual in the fact that the bed is blessed by the priest, but here the detail adds to the suggestion of death or disaster, and becomes another warning sign to the reader. May's worst nightmare approaches in the shape of her new husband January who takes her 'faste in armes' the minute they are alone. Both the quick rhythm of the lines and the repetition of 'And' suggest the sudden and irrevocable rush towards an embrace for which May is stoically prepared. Everything happens at once. She is 'broght abedde' as if unwilling, 'And' once the priest has blessed the bridal chamber everyone disappears before, with another 'And', January takes her in his arms. At this point the rhythm slows as he embraces 'His fresshe May, his paradys, his make'. His lovely wife, young as her name – so evocative of spring – suggests, is his entirely and he sets about making love to her with a careful and deliberate activity reflected in the list of verbs as well as the structure of the following lines, an activity which is in direct contrast to May's passive 'stille as stoon'. January lulls her, kisses her, 'rubbeth hire aboute hir tendre face', and 'laboureth' until dawn.

Let us look more closely at the sequence of events. January begins slowly as the pauses intimate: 'He lulleth hire; he kisseth hire ful ofte'. His attempts to put May at her ease are clearly unsuccessful. On the one hand he speaks to his reluctant and inexperienced bride with apparently thoughtful tenderness. He apologises for what he is about to do with 'Allas!', and a fear that he might 'yow greetly offende'. Implicit in his words is a promise that he is an expert in these matters, a craftsman or a 'werkman', and he invites her to recall that a good workman never hurries the job but takes his time, takes care, exactly as January will, an intention made explicit in the line 'This wol be doon at leyser parfitly'. He explains that this is no sin for they are now joined in 'trewe wedlok' and might 'pleye' at their leisure, 'For in oure actes we mowe do no synne'.

Consequently his lovemaking lasts all night and is the cause of much enjoyment to him as witnessed by his post-honeymoon behaviour. The following morning he sits up in his bed to take his breakfast, singing loudly and clearly before kissing 'his wyf' and lecherously ('wantown') teasing her. Once again the light rhythm and repetition of 'And' underscores January's activity as he does this. Presumably May passively accepts his behaviour for there is no mention of her or of her reaction. January himself feels years younger, and is as frisky as a colt, full of 'ragerye', chattering away like a magpie. The animal imagery is ambiguous, both emphasising his base lust and yet intimating that it is natural.

What then of May? Other details point to a less than enthusiastic reception. Again we notice the long list of verbs. Here they clarify the fact that it is January who is an active participant and not she. We are told that 'he kisseth hire ful ofte', 'He rubbeth' her face and 'kiste his wyf', 'he sang', and 'Thus laboureth he til that the day gan dawe'. It is a repetition that underscores the fact that May is only the passive recipient of an activity in which her husband takes enormous pleasure. May is no more than another of January's possessions, an idea indicated by the frequency of the personal pronoun 'his'. She is 'his paradys, his make', 'his wyf', 'His fresshe May', and, of course, 'my spouse'. It is a language that belies the mutual bliss ostensibly apparent in his insistence upon the *pair* of them when he speaks of the sex act within marriage.

January reminds her that 'we tweye' are joined together, that 'we been inne' the 'yok' of marriage where 'we pleye' at our leisure. He adds 'we han leve to pleye us by the lawe' for 'in oure actes we mowe do no synne'. Here the pronouns actually point to the fact that, by law, January can now do with his wife as he likes. When he says 'we' he really means 'I'. This serves as a reminder that she must be prepared to suffer his attentions at all times for by 'the lawe' she must now submit to his sexual advances. January's apparent eulogy to marriage as 'trewe wedlok' and a 'blessed...yok' has the effect of suggesting that the union might bring more advantage to the husband than the wife. In the same way his comment that a man may do no sin with his own wife, 'Ne hurte hymselven with his owene knyf', reinforces his belief that May is his sexual plaything. It is also a misinterpretation of marital 'law' as outlined in the *Parson's Tale* where, in fact, the phrase reads as 'a man may sleen hymself with his owene knyf'; there the Parson reiterates standard theological teaching which warns that pleasure in the sex act for its own sake, even when legitimated by marriage, remains a sin.

January's performance is more than ultimately blasphemous – it is repugnant. The cumulative effect of the details mentioned so far is bolstered by the sly inclusion of other lines designed to stir revulsion. When January kisses May reference is made to his harsh and bristly beard, 'Lyk to the skyn of houndfyssh, sharp as brere – ', which he rubs all over his wife's 'tendre face' even as he apologises for what he is about to do to her. His apparent concern about offending her is negated in his subsequent comment that 'Er tyme come that I wil doun descende'. This sounds remarkably like a salacious threat, almost an attempt to frighten his virgin bride and excite himself. It is a terrifying prospect and one reiterated by his promise to perform 'at leyser parfitly'.

Similarly, January's behaviour the next morning might be read as a deliberate reminder of *his* enjoyment as he revels in his delight, singing loudly and having fun. The description of his 'slakke skyn', that fold of skin at the neck of an old man, his 'nekke lene', and the sight of him sitting up in his shirt and his night cap, all remind both us and May of his age. Their union is portrayed as an unnatural one despite their names, so suggestive of the seasons and the natural world. The mere thought of January's physical appearance evokes a shudder of repulsion so that the question implicit in 'God woot what that May thoughte in hir herte' is answered even before the closing line of the passage with the comment that, distinctly unimpressed, 'She preyseth nat his pleyyng worth a bene'.

Once again it is the choice of detail and vocabulary that is revealing, but only when we carefully examine the structure of the passage. Then we see how ideas accumulate or are contrasted with each other, and can judge the tone of the piece. In addition, we have already seen how Chaucer's themes and ideas might be revealed to us by placing an extract in its wider context – in relation to speaker, to other sections of a tale, or to other tales themselves. These techniques all prove useful with this passage.

Without doubt this portrayal of married love is firmly on the side of the female. How far is its view applicable to other things you might have read – the Wife's comments, for example? Earlier we explored an ambiguous description of Alison from the *Miller's Tale*. Is Chaucer sympathetic to her or not? Other factors inevitably cast some doubt upon the ideas expressed in this passage as a standard by which we might 'read' other presentations of women. Who speaks here – Chaucer or the narrator, the Merchant? How does a reading of the complete tale alter your opinion, especially concerning 'fresshe

May'? Whatever your conclusions this remains a fascinating portrayal.

At this point it might be interesting to examine a section from the *Nun's Priest's Tale* which presents a very different portrait of married life. It occurs just after Chauntecleer has decided he will finally abandon his lengthy and authoritative homily on dreams. Bearing in mind what has already been revealed through the presentation of Chauntecleer's character, what attitude towards women is suggested here?

> "Now let us speke of myrthe, and stynte al this.
> Madame Pertelote, so have I blis,
> Of o thyng God hath sent me large grace;
> For whan I se the beautee of youre face,
> Ye been so scarlet reed aboute youre yen
> It maketh al my dred for to dyen;
> For al so siker as *In principio*,
> *Mulier est hominis confusio* –
> Madame, the sentence of this Latyn is,
> 'Womman is mannes joye and al his blis.'
> For whan I feele a-nyght your softe syde –
> Al be it that I may nat on yow ryde,
> For that oure perche is maad so narwe, allas –
> I am so ful of joye and of solas,
> That I diffye bothe sweven and dreem."
> And with that word he fley doun fro the beem,
> For it was day, and eke his hennes alle,
> And with a chuk he gan hem for to calle,
> For he hadde founde a corn, lay in the yerd.
> Real he was, he was namoore aferd.
> He fethered Pertelote twenty tyme,
> And trad hire eke as ofte, er it was pryme.
> He looketh as it were a grym leoun,
> And on his toos he rometh up and doun;
> Hym deigned nat to sette his foot to grounde.
> He chukketh whan he hath a corn yfounde,
> And to hym rennen thanne his wyves alle.
> Thus roial, as a prince is in his halle,
> Leve I this Chauntecleer in his pasture
> ...

(VII, ll.3157–85)

Chauntecleer turns from his homily on dream lore to 'speke of myrthe', or, more precisely, of Pertelote, the light of his life. Once again the terminology used in connection with this beast is extravagant and courtly. Chauntecleer is depicted as a 'grym leoun', king of all animals, roaming around his yard or kingdom 'on his toos', for he is so proud that 'Hym deigned nat to sette his foot to grounde'. He is master of his own small universe. When he finds some grain, he calls and his 'wyves' all run to him. He is termed 'Real', or royal, while the narrator notes he is 'Thus roial, as a prince is in his halle'.

At the same time Chauntecleer acts out the role of a courtly lover. He calls his favourite hen 'Madame Pertelote' and 'Madame', praising 'the beautee of youre face', and the scarlet ring around her eye. She is his grace from God, his 'blis', and when he looks upon her he dreads to die. His language is extravagant and his sentiments highly dramatic.

Pertelote's beauty inspires him to dismiss his fears, to defy any dream he might have had, to forget it, and walk up and down the yard exactly as Pertelote had earlier urged when she insisted that his fearful dreams were not portents but due only to indigestion. So, Chauntecleer flies down from his roosting place, gathers his hens around him, eats the corn he finds, and behaves totally naturally; he

> 'fethered Pertelote twenty tyme,
> And trad hire eke as ofte, er it was pryme.'

Once again these details call attention to several important issues. The inflated language and depiction of Chauntecleer as a courtly lover, prince of his world, is undercut by a more prosaic word choice in a reminder that this same courtly hero is also just a simple farmyard animal.

The first part of the passage consists of two lengthy and complex sentences carefully structured by a series of semi-colons and logical connections such as 'For al', 'For whan', 'Al be it', 'For that', and 'so ful.../That I...' Similarly the sentence beginning 'For whan I feel a-nyght' is interrupted by three lines of parentheses. His attitude towards his 'wife' is both loving and sensual. Though disappointed that their night-time perch is too narrow to allow them to copulate,

Chauntecleer is nevertheless enchanted by the sensation of her 'softe syde' against his own, a feeling that leaves him 'so ful of joye and of solas'.

The remainder of the extract is a contrast to this pompous speech, detailing instead Chauntecleer's behaviour. The language is more loosely structured and focuses upon the homely as well as natural actions. Chauntecleer refers to 'oure perche' and comments on 'his hennes', how 'with a chuk he gan hem for to calle', how he 'chukketh' when he 'founde a corn, lay in the yerd', or how he 'fley doun fro the beem' and 'rometh up and doun', or else 'fethered' his wife, 'trad hire' many times before noon. As a mere beast Chauntecleer cannot represent a human husband, and cannot be expected to be subject to human law insisting on monogamy. The fact that he copulates twenty times in one morning with Pertelote and has several 'wives' reinforces this. Yet, at the same time, other details and word choice seem to suggest that the relationship between Chauntecleer and Pertelote *is* symbolic of marital relations.

Chauntecleer is the dominant male, master of all he surveys. He is even described as 'roial', a 'prince', while his earlier words on dream lore are spoken with the authority ascribed to both text and the masculine. He dismisses Pertelote's refusal to take his dream seriously and rejects her common-sense advice with a wealth of textual evidence. She apparently accepts this. Yet Chauntecleer *does* follow her suggestions and begins to walk around the yard as she had advised. Refusing to be hen-pecked, he is in fact just that, and this amusing little episode suddenly takes on greater significance as an example of human marital relationships, an entirely natural and convincing portrait of how some men and women behave together.

It is a concern that reveals itself elsewhere in the passage too. As we noticed earlier, Chauntecleer's speech is extravagant and courtly. In the midst of his eulogy to Pertelote's beauty, he is reminded of the Latin tag that 'Woman is the source of man's ruin', a saying that he misconstrues as 'Womman is mannes joye and al his blis'. Twice he refers to Pertelote as 'blis' as well as his 'joye' and 'solas'. He is filled with a love that takes its expression both in flattering endearments and sexuality, 'fethering' her often and taking pleasure in the feel of her 'softe syde' next to him at night. Their love is both courtly and romantic, and yet entirely natural. Sex and love are not separated, as they might have been in the courtly romance tradition, and the sex act is a frequent one. What do you think Chaucer is trying to suggest about love in this example? Compare it to his treatment of courtly love in the *Knight's Tale* or think about the way in which Nicholas, in the *Miller's Tale*, wooed Alison with romantic and elegant words at exactly the same time as he grabbed hold of her 'queynte'. Possibly Chaucer is poking fun at an outdated and idealistic ritual of love, an ideal like other medieval precepts about love that ignored its natural physical expression, tried to deny its existence, or even, in the case of Nicholas's version of courtly love, used this form of courtship as a means to an end.

Yet, however natural and loving the relationship between Chauntecleer and Pertelote might be, in human terms it remains almost sacrilegious when set against ideals put forward by clerical and other authoritative teaching. For a human to place so much emphasis upon another as 'blis' or 'solas' is in defiance of medieval teaching which stressed the false vanity of such a worldly relationship. Instead, thoughts were to be directed to God, an idea adding a neat irony to Chauntecleer's assertion that it is God who has sent him the 'grace' of Pertelote's beauty. Similarly, the sex act was intended ideally (though obviously not in practice) for procreation alone and not for pure lusty enjoyment, while the idea that woman is equated with joy is in direct contradiction to authoritative teaching representing her as a source of temptation and ruin, and blaming her for the expulsion from the Garden of Eden. For further elaboration of these views, read the *Parson's Tale* or the opening to the *Merchant's Tale*.

Thus Chaucer is able to use this story to offer yet another perspective on the issues of love, sex and marriage. A reminder that the view expressed here is that of a cockerel is never very far from the surface, but in the wider context of both this individual tale and the *Tales* itself it is given a particular resonance.

The next extract, from the *Wife of Bath's Prologue*, also focuses upon men and women to reveal a gap between ideal and practice only hinted at in our previous passage. As you read it you might like to consider what it reveals about medieval marriage and relationships between the sexes. Once again you will need to look closely at word choice, and at the movement or shape of the extract. In this concluding section of her lengthy *Prologue* the Wife tells of marriage to her fifth husband, her beloved Jankyn. Just prior to the extract here, he has been recounting a long list of anti-feminist authorities from his favourite book.

And whan I saugh he wolde nevere fyne
To reden on this cursed book al nyght,
Out of his book, right as he radde, and eke
I with my fest so took hym on the cheke
That in oure fyr he fil bakward adoun.
And up he stirte as dooth a wood leoun,
And with his fest he smoot me on the heed
That in the floor I lay as I were deed.
And whan he saugh how stille that I lay,
He was agast and wolde han fled his way,
Til atte laste out of my swogh I breyde.
'O! hastow slayn me, false theef?' I seyde,
'And for my land thus hastow mordred me?
Er I be deed, yet wole I kisse thee.'
And neer he cam, and kneled faire adoun,
And seyde, 'Deere suster Alisoun,
As help me God, I shal thee nevere smyte!
That I have doon, it is thyself to wyte.
Foryeve it me, and that I thee biseke!'
And yet eftsoones, I hitte hym on the cheke,
And seyde, 'Theef, thus muchel am I wreke;
Now wol I dye, I may no lenger speke.'
But atte laste, with muchel care and wo,
We fille acorded by us selven two.
He yaf me al the bridel in myn hond,
To han the governance of hous and lond,
And of his tonge, and of his hond also;
And made hym brenne his book anon right tho.
And whan that I hadde geten unto me,
By maistrie, al the soveraynetee,
And that he seyde, 'Myn owene trewe wyf,
Do as thee lust the terme of al thy lyf;
Keep thyn honour, and keep eek myn estaat' –

After that day we hadden never debaat.

(III (D), ll.788–822)

Once again a quick glance at the text reveals clusters or patterns which offer clues about its content. This time, attempt to search for these yourself. Perhaps you could focus upon the predominance of active verbs or the forceful dialogue set against the calmer, more courteous speech of the closing lines. This last section too has a selection of words like 'bridel', 'maistrie', and 'soveraynetee'. What do they suggest to you?

The passage opens in dramatic style with the Wife's response to the challenge implicit in Jankyn's earlier monologue. Rather than submit, to behave as an obedient and passive wife should, she rises up in anger once she realises that he is set upon reading 'this cursed book al nyght', and suddenly, as he reads, she rips out three of the pages. Not content with this she punches him in the face so that he falls backwards into the fire. The Wife tells us this in a long sentence, in a rush of excitement, for this is the turning point in their relationship.

Jankyn is furious and, like 'a wood leoun', he springs to his feet, striking her on the head 'with his fest'. Alison lies on the floor 'as I were deed'. The terrified Jankyn plans to flee until she suddenly awakens from her 'swogh' and rails against him, insulting him with cries of 'false theef', accusing him of trying to 'slayn me', to murder her.

The opening half of this extract is lively and dramatic, full of action. The scene depicted is a literal battle between the sexes. The Wife's actions are astonishing; she refuses to be cowed by the citation of these authorities. Instead her response is a refusal to be degraded or psychologically battered into submission. Unable to refute the authority of a written text, she responds to Jankyn's words with violent action. She literally strikes a blow for herself and for her sex too. The image with which we are presented is highly comic, but it conceals a much deeper issue.

The pair violently berate each other and the Wife concludes her brief tirade with an accusation that Jankyn has attempted to kill her 'for my land'. Here she inadvertently reveals her view of marriage as a purely business transaction, a mercenary alliance entered into for personal gain where love is an irrelevancy. (In what way might this relate to the previous passage?) Perhaps at this moment Alison recognises that as an elderly widow her main attraction is her wealth. With this in mind she plots revenge for his blow, adding, 'Er I be deed, yet wol I kisse thee', and enticing Jankyn nearer. Somewhat to our surprise, his response is an affectionate one. Kneeling beside her he calls her 'Deere suster Alisoun', begs for forgiveness, swears 'I shal thee nevere smyt!' He also blames her for his action. Just as the tone threatens to become sentimental, as we briefly imagine an idyllic ending and romantic *rapprochement*, our expectations are shattered by Alison's bathetic and highly entertaining reply:

> And yet eftsoones, I hitte hym on the cheke,
> And seyde, 'Theef, thus muchel am I wreke!;

Once again her dismissal of all words, written or spoken, is dramatic and uncompromising. This is her violent revenge, one harking back to an extract discussed earlier where she advised other women to do as she does here and ensure that they always strike the first blow in the 'werre' between men and women. A direct contrast is struck and maintained. The first contrast is the gulf between men and women. The second concerns the masculine authority vested in the written and spoken word which is set against another opposition, namely the active, the literal, or even the violent expressed in the female's fight back. The war in which Alison engages is at once both comic and deadly serious.

Its resolution is swiftly passed over, however. The Wife merely refers to 'muchel care and wo' before taking us to its happy ending. She makes Jankyn burn his book in symbolic destruction of anti-feminist orthodoxy, and claims for herself all 'maistrie' and 'al the soveraynetee'. Jankyn surrenders his traditional power and 'yaf me the bridel in myn hond'. He permits his wife to rule entirely, to govern the house, the land and himself. His words are loving, 'Myn owene trewe wyf', and invite her to behave exactly as she pleases so long as she 'keep thyn honour, and keep eek myn estaat – '. At this point Alison breaks off to add the short simple conclusion 'After that day we hadden never debaat'. It is an almost fairy-tale ending, an idyllic 'happy-ever-after' state that, emphasised by the brevity of the line, closes down all discussion, brooks no argument, and leaves little room for alternatives. Her words imply that for Alison this arrangement is personally satisfying, and they also preface the tale she is about to tell.

Her actions clearly go beyond entertainment. What is Chaucer's intent here? The Wife's depiction of a marital battleground and struggle for power is itself a damning indictment of medieval marriage. In an effort to alter a situation in which women were subordinate and suppressed, Alison literally fights back. Her response to a range of anti-feminist propaganda, attitudes instilled by the weight of written and verbal masculine authority, is to use violence in an attempt to destroy both the words (literally as she tears the pages of the book) and their effect. Thus Chaucer opens up for analysis, exploration, and even criticism, the institution of marriage and the relationship between men and women. In theory Alison ought to correspond to the ideal and be a subservient wife; in practice her refusal is uncompromising.

Once again though the Wife is but one voice. Her ideas are no more or less definitive than the issues presented via Jankyn's book, nor her portrait any more clearcut than any other in the *Tales*. The question of whether Alison is harmlessly amusing or a subversive monster is perhaps ultimately unanswerable. The picture of 'woman' presented in Jankyn's reading material is of a sexually insatiable virago, a potential murderess without shame or loyalty, or an angry and wicked scold. It is this fear of women that Chaucer's Wife of Bath both encapsulates and defuses as we laugh at her antics that in themselves ape the stereotype. Some would suggest that she responds to the anti-feminist tradition by inverting the ideal of the meek and mild wife to 'become' the woman just described. In this extract she *is* angry, she *is* violent, though ironically she accuses Jankyn of trying to murder her. She adopts a masculine role by accepting the 'bridel' and attempting to dominate. Is she to be vilified or praised for this? Is her response perhaps the only one available to women like her? It is an open question.

The next extract may help you to make up your mind. It too

is from the *Wife's Prologue* and returns us to the issue of anti-feminism. As you read try to set it against the passage we have just explored.

He hadde a book that gladly, nyght and day,
For his desport he wolde rede alway;
He cleped it Valerie and Theofraste,
At which book he lough alwey ful faste.
And eek ther was somtyme a clerk at Rome,
A cardinal, that highte Seint Jerome,
That made a book agayn Jovinian;
In which book eek ther was Tertulan,
Crisippus, Trotula, and Helowys,
That was abbesse nat fer fro Parys,
And eek the Parables of Salomon,
Ovides Art, and bookes many on,
And alle thise were bounden in o volume.
And every nyght and day was his custume,
Whan he hadde leyser and vacacioun
From oother wordly occupacioun,
To reden on this book of wikked wyves.
He knew of hem mo legendes and lyves
Than been of goode wyves in the Bible.
For trusteth wel, it is an impossible
That any clerk wol speke good of wyves,
But if it be of hooly seintes lyves,
Ne of noon oother womman never the mo.
Who peyntede the leon, tel me who?
By God, if wommen hadde writen stories,
As clerkes han withinne hire oratories,
They wolde han writen of men moore wikked-/nesse
Than al the mark of Adam may redresse.

(III (D), ll.669–96)

It is easy to spot the main focus of this passage by the repetition of phrases denoting the female, things like 'wikked wyves', 'goode wyves', 'good of wyves', 'oother womman', or simply 'wommen'. This terminology is set against references to reading and to clerks, while the list of names – Jovinian, Jerome, Ovid, Solomon, Valerie, and Theofraste amongst others – indicates a concern with authority which forms the basis of Jankyn's 'evidence'.

The Wife begins by telling us that her husband had 'a book' that 'he wolde rede alwey'. She immediately signals that the content of this book is distressing to her while the activity of his reading is itself underscored as a masculine and exclusive one; she is ignored while Jankyn reads 'nyght and day'. What is worse is that he apparently spends his time laughing at it. Whether he is genuinely amused by it or admires its content is irrelevant. The point is that Alison is not allowed to share the joke, and is forced either to watch him read or listen to the extracts he chooses to read out loud. Her exclusion is reinforced with the later repetition of 'every nyght and day', and her remark that whenever 'he hadde leyser and vacacioun' he settled down 'To reden on this book of wikked wyves'.

The content of this book is even more disturbing. Jankyn has 'bounden in o volume' a vast array of material and other books ranging far and wide in terms of authorship. The flurry of commas intimates that the agitated Wife recounts some of them with scarcely a pause, the names piling up in a long list as in the following example:

> ...ther was Tertulan,
> Crisippus, Trotula, and Helowys,
> That was abbesse nat fer fro Parys,
> And eek the parables of Salomon,
> Ovides Art, and bookes many on,
> And alle thise...

They are fleeting references but all immediately meaningful to her medieval audience as largely anti-feminist authorities.

Alison's distress is clear from the beginning. Look at the length of her early sentences, and the repetition of 'and' seen in the line beginning 'And all thise were bounden in o volume...'

The tone is set right at the start with 'Valerie and Theofraste', male authors of works attacking marriage. As far as Alison is concerned the entire volume is dedicated to speaking ill of women, devoted to tales of 'wikked wyves', and her own husband, like all clerks, is an expert in the field of misogyny, knowing 'mo legendes and lyves' about evil women than he does 'of goode wyves in the Bible'.

Here the Wife cites one single reference to set against the weight of Jankyn's well-documented belief, the highest she can think of – the Bible. Yet her faith in it is limited as she implies in her comment that 'it is an impossible' for any clerk to speak positively of women unless citing saints' legends, a near-impossible ideal for any woman (or man!) to emulate. Of 'oother womman' nothing is heard.

As the names of these authorities build up into the crushing weight of an ideology apparently supported by 'any clerk' or the power of the Church (remember that 'clerk' might mean a learned man or a man of the Church), we can almost feel Alison's barely suppressed pain. It is an emotion intimated in the double negative of the line 'ne of noon oother womman never the mo' and her sudden outburst into the question 'Who peyntede the leon?' Who, she demands, 'tel me who?' in urgent despair. Her question opens up the possibility of an alternative viewpoint building upon her earlier remark that clerks invariably fail to speak well of women. Her oath is a heartfelt one; she declares 'By God, if wommen hadde writen' the material contained in chapels all over the land, and presumably referred to by all learned men, then the situation might have been very different, for women 'wolde han writen of men moore wikked-/nesse' than anything the male sex produced, in order to redress the balance.

The strength of Alison's concluding remark stems from the depth of its emotion. It is not simply that she is genuinely hurt by Jankyn's neglect of her, but that in itself that preoccupation with his book symbolises the division between them as man and woman. Jankyn has access to a knowledge that bestows power upon him as a male. It provides him with a wealth of authoritative material that he can, and later does, wield as a highly damaging weapon in the sex 'war'.

At the same time the attitudes it disseminates must inevitably permeate his thinking. Moreover it is an authority vested solely in the male, in those with access to learning or Church office, and those able to read and write. In contrast Alison, and all women whom on this occasion she represents, is denied that power in all its forms, and it is precisely this which renders so poignant her belief that women might write enough to rival any man's collection. For ordinary medieval women did not, on the whole, write. Instead, they might be perceived as inevitably affected by the zealous drive to turn them into ideals of femininity in much the same way that a clever and subtle advertising campaign might insinuate itself into the minds of the public with the potential to alter beliefs or affect behaviour. Alison's personal anecdote, about the fact that Jankyn continually reads and enjoys anti-feminist material, drives home the message that such thinking and such ideals easily pervade everyday life and practice. She has no legitimate or realistic means of having her voice heard as a woman and neither does she fully comprehend the issues involved. She only wishes that she could strike back in the same way and write similar stories about men. Yet it is a futile hope, as well she knows, and she can only bewail the gulf between them.

The extent to which Alison fails to understand completely the pertinence of her remarks is perhaps more fully indicated by the remainder of her *Prologue* which follows this passage. Read the two sections in conjunction and try to see how the wider context of the whole *Prologue* helps to form your ideas about individual sections. Here Chaucer's focus upon the prevailing misogyny of his time is entirely clear even if his own perspective is not. It is a theme to which he returns in other tales where, once again, alternatives are apparently proposed.

III: EXPERIENCE VERSUS AUTHORITY – THE *MILLER'S TALE*, THE *PARSON'S TALE* AND THE *WIFE OF BATH'S PROLOGUE*

The next extract takes us onto a different topic. It occurs in the *Miller's Tale*, just as John the carpenter's curiosity about his lodger Nicholas's refusal to leave his room overwhelms him exactly as Nicholas had hoped, and prepares us for the plot outcome. What impression of John is given, and what does this suggest about attitudes towards learning and knowledge? Again look carefully at the vocabulary associated with John as well as the way in which the passage is structured.

> This sely carpenter hath greet merveyle
> Of Nicholas, or what thyng myghte hym eyle,
> And seyde, "I am adrad, by Seint Thomas,
> It stondeth nat aright with Nicholas.
> God shilde that he deyde sodeynly!
> This world is now ful tikel, sikerly.
> I saugh today a cors yborn to chirche
> That now, on Monday last, I saugh hym / wirche.
> "Go up," quod he unto his knave anoon,
> "Clepe at his dore, or knokke with a stoon.
> Looke how it is, and tel me boldely."
> This knave gooth hym up ful sturdily,
> And at the chambre dore whil that he stood,
> He cride and knokked as that he were wood,
> "What, how! What do ye, maister Nicholay?
> How may ye slepen al the longe day?"
> But al for noght; he herde nat a word.
> An hole he foond, ful lowe upon a bord,
> Ther as the cat was wont in for to crepe,
> And at that hole he looked in ful depe,
> And at the laste he hadde of hym a sight.
> This Nicholas sat evere capyng upright,
> As he has kiked on the newe moone.
> Adoun he gooth, and tolde his maister soone
> In what array he saugh this ilke man.
> This carpenter to blessen hym bigan,
> And seyde, "Help us, Seinte Frydeswyde!
> A man woot litel what hym shal bityde.
> This man is falle, with his astromye,
> In some woodnesse or in som agonye.
> I thoghte ay wel how that it sholde be!
> Men sholde nat knowe of Goddes pryvetee.
> Ye, blessed be alwey a lewed man
> That noght but oonly his bileve kan!
> So ferde another clerk with astromye;
> He walked in the feeldes for to prye
> Upon the sterres, what ther sholde bifalle,

Til he was in a marle-pit yfalle;
He saugh nat that.

(I (A), ll.3423–61)

The ambiguity of Chaucer's stance concerning the issue of learning is implied in the repetitive terminology used to describe John. He is 'This sely carpenter', a word that might mean either foolish or innocent. That he is an uneducated, even ignorant, man is suggested by his speech. It is full of oaths, but not oaths in the coarse manner of a character like the Miller. John's references to 'by Seint Thomas', 'God shilde', 'Goddes pryvetee', and 'Help us, Seinte Frydeswyde!' border on the superstitious. Implicit within them is total trust in some external force which guides and shapes human lives, an entity with superior knowledge that will protect him and those around him. At the same time John's attitude towards the sly and clever student Nicholas is one of genuine concern for his well-being, mingled with a fearful admiration for what he perceives as his learning. We are highly entertained by both John's behaviour and his beliefs.

Events move on. John wonders why no one has seen Nicholas all weekend. He worries about what 'myghte hym eyle' and is 'adrad' that 'It stondeth nat aright' with him. God forbid, he cries, that he should die suddenly! In a panic he sends his servant to investigate, urging him to rouse Nicholas by calling out or knocking on his door with a stone. The servant obeys, hammering on the door 'as that he were wood', but to no avail. Dramatic tension rises emphasised by the pause or caesura of the line 'But al for noght; he herde nat a word.' Then comes the comic spectacle of the servant crouching down to peer through the cat flap.

The sight of Nicholas bolt upright in bed, eyes fixed on the heavens as though 'he had kiked on the newe moone', is extremely amusing, even more so when he rushes down to tell his master. It forms the climax of the passage as John's worst fears are apparently realised. John's excessive reaction is based on pure terror, and not solely for Nicholas's welfare. Earlier, suggesting his own simple ignorance, he shakes his head in sorrow at the world's instability. It 'is now ful tikel, sikerly' he says and offers an anecdote, apparently based on personal experience, to prove it. He has empirical evidence of his belief for 'I saugh today a cors yborn to chirche'; last Monday that same man was alive and at work. This is the core of John's learning, an everyday almost proverbial set of beliefs founded in a faith in God and the saints and demonstrated by his daily lived experience. It does not stem from books and, as such, has little recognised authority. In any case John fears that type of learning, and has no trust in it as exemplified by the concluding part of the extract.

John's anxiety for Nicholas, and about the world in general, reaches new heights at this point. The carpenter's faith is vested in a superstitious reliance upon what everyday life can prove to him or show him. So, when he hears that Nicholas is sitting up in bed in a trance and gazing at the moon, he *knows* that disaster is upon his friend. John's concern is touching but it never crosses his mind that appearances might deceive. Instead he crosses himself, calls on the saints for help, and blames Nicholas's learning for his bizarre behaviour. He says that it is 'his astromye' that has caused him to suffer agonies or go mad and, just as we might expect, offers yet another lived or 'proven' example to support his view.

He cites the case of the clerk who, out walking in the fields, gazed so intently upon the night sky and the 'sterres' that he fell into a clay pit. The audience is here forced to suppress laughter as John indicates his complete faith in this account as visual evidence and a warning sign to all. Both the line break and the pause emphasise his seriousness:

> 'Til he was in marle-pit yfalle;
> He saugh nat that.'

We realise that John trusts in a world that he can see and touch, one that he believes demonstrates things to him or offers concrete examples. He puts his faith in the literal, in what he sees, and not in books or in words, in non-tangible evidence. In short, John's belief is that knowledge is something to be avoided at all costs. He has fully expected that Nicholas's learning would lead to adversity, declaring 'I thoghte ay wel how that it sholde be!' John puts his trust in simple faith for

> 'Ye, blessed be alwey a lewed man
> That noght but oonly his bileve kan!'

His exclamation underlines the strength of his foolish (or simplistic!) and amusing comment. He insists that 'Men sholde nat knowe of Goddes pryvetee', and that certain areas of knowledge are best kept closed. It is faith and experience, not learning, upon which he depends. That Nicholas has broken what for John is a taboo is a matter of mingled awe and gleeful triumph that his own belief has been vindicated, that he, simple John, knows better than this clever clerk.

What this amusing extract reveals, of course, is John's readiness to be gulled by the power of Nicholas's apparent learning. At first glance it appears to suggest that Chaucer too participates in the laughter at John's expense. Yet John remains an easy target and Nicholas's elaborate plot is not only devoted merely to the satisfaction of his sexual appetite but even seems unnecessary, especially given that Alison is such a willing partner. In whose learning should we place our trust?

Chaucer draws our attention to two different kinds of learning here – the book-based knowledge of Nicholas, and the visual, lived experience of John. The structure of this passage cleverly aids this division. It begins with John's fears, a sense that all is not well with his friend because no one has seen him. That fear is 'proved' correct by visual evidence, the sight of a half-crazed Nicholas glimpsed through the door. John interprets this according to his own mistrust of learning. The remainder of the extract is devoted to John's justification for what he believes, shown by his references to similar situations he has either witnessed or heard of. Thus his false premise is demonstrated to his own satisfaction by the world at large. Yet the reader knows better, and it is of course this lack of imagination and his reliance upon the literal which is his undoing in the plot.

Once again an important issue manifests itself ambiguously. The *Miller's Tale* offers one perspective on the question of learning, authority and experience, as does the extract from the *Wife of Bath's Prologue* which follows our next passage. This is taken from the *Parson's Tale* and offers a very different kind of learning as its example, that of clerical masculine knowledge. Here Chaucer explores what is implicit in the effects of this type of knowledge and its transmission, particularly with regard to attitudes towards women and towards marriage. As you read it, try and search for key words or phrases, for a pattern in the use of terminology, as well as focusing upon the structure of its content. What sort of writing is this and how are you able to recognise it?

> Now how that a womman sholde be subget to hire housbonde, that telleth Seint Peter. First, in obedience./ And eek, as seith the decree, a womman that is wyf, as longe as she is a wyf, she hath noon auctoritee to swere ne to bere witnesse withoute leve of hir housbonde, that is hire lord; algate, he sholde be so by resoun./ She shold eek serven hym in alle honestee, and been attempree of hire array. I woot wel that they sholde setten hire entente to plesen hir housbondes, but nat by hire queyntise of array./ Seint Jerome seith that "wyves that been apparailled in silk and in precious purpre ne mowe nat clothen hem in Jhesu Crist." Loke what seith Seint John eek in thys matere?/ Seint Gregorie eek seith that " No wight seketh precious array but oonly for veyne glorie, to been honoured the moore biforn the peple."/ It is a greet folye, a womman to have a fair array outward and in hirself be foul inward./ A wyf sholde eek be mesurable in lookynge and in berynge and in lawghynge, and discreet in alle hire wordes and hire dedes./ And aboven alle worldly thyng she sholde loven hire housbonde with al hir herte, and to hym be trewe of hir body./ So sholde an housbonde eek be to his wyf. For sith that al the body is the housbondes, so sholde hire herte been, or elles ther is bitwixte hem two, as in that, no parfit mariage./ Thanne shal men understonde that for thre thynges a man and his wyf flesshly mowen assemble. The firste is in entente of engendrure of children to the service of God, for certes that is the cause final of matrimoyne./ Another cause is to yelden everich of hem to oother the dette of hire bodies, for neither of hem hath power of his owene body. The thridde is for to eschewe leccherye and vileynye. The ferthe is for sothe deedly synne./
>
> (X (I), ll.928–39)

This is the final tale in the entire collection, a serious and lengthy sermon told by the humble Parson. The fact that it is written in prose rather than verse denotes it as entirely sober, a considered piece of 'sentence' and not the coarse frivolity of the fabliaux or stories like them. The contest ends then on a serious note, in 'ernest'; this is not a tale told in 'game' or one of the merry things the Host calls for so frequently. There is not really space to do justice to this complex and challenging work but you should certainly ponder the question of why such a story is apparently chosen as the last word in the *Tales*. Undoubtedly it is, in part, a mirror through which other tales might be reflected, and certainly the brief extract chosen here casts an uncomfortable light on much of our explorations so far. Is it intended as the definitive final word though, do you think, or as a closure? Have the multiplicities and ambiguities of previous perspectives really been reduced to this? This is something for you to think about. What bearing, if any, does this passage have on what you have seen so far in the other extracts we have considered, or in your own reading?

These words are spoken by the fictional Parson, a man of lowly religious office who, in contrast to characters like the Pardoner and even the Prioress, takes his occupation extremely seriously. We straightaway spot the sermon style of this piece. It begins with a bald statement, holds up an ideal, not for us to examine but to accept. It is an assertion of 'fact' that brooks no argument but simply and plainly states its intent and immediately supports it with an unequivocal, masculine authority: 'Now how that a womman sholde be subget to hire housbonde, that telleth Seint Peter.'

The Parson then moves to expand and reinforce this idea by offering clear evidence or authority to prove it, and by using a series of phrases designed to indicate to his audience what he is in the process of expounding. There are none of the rhetorical tricks used by the Pardoner. Instead, what is said is plain and unadorned; in effect, the content is left to speak for itself. 'First', he offers, then 'and eek', 'Thanne shal men understonde', 'The firste is in...', 'another cause is...', 'The thridde is...,' and finally 'The ferthe is...' Clarity is his watchword. His authorities are cited with complete and unthinking conviction according to what 'seith the decree', and include the saints Peter, John, Gregory and Jerome. Usually the speaker paraphrases his sources suggesting that they are firmly embedded in his memory. Some, however, are quoted directly to give added weight to his ideas as in 'Seint Jerome seith that "wyves that been apparailled in silk and in precious purpre ne mowe nat clothen hem in Jhesu Crist".' A similar example is given from St Gregory. The effect is to make the Parson sound learned but also irritates by hinting that this is a man whose mind is firmly closed to other possibilities, one who can only parrot the dogma he has been taught.

The Parson's story is intended to reiterate a lesson or an ideal. Here he preaches on how to avoid the sin of 'luxurie' or lust. He is a stern and uncompromising teacher as evidenced by the prevalence of direct statement and the repetition of 'sholde'. He declares that a husband 'sholde be so', that women 'sholde' set out to please their men, that 'A wyf sholde' behave in the way he suggests, that 'she sholde' love her husband, and even that 'So sholde' a husband love his wife. Similarly, a woman's body belongs to her spouse and 'so sholde hire herte been'.

The Parson carefully prescribes a code of behaviour through a series of assertions, backed by authority, which close down all discussion. One small phrase in the opening line of this extract sets the tone for what is to come; it is all about 'how that a womman sholde be'. Though the Parson appears to speak of both men and women, it is interesting to note the emphasis upon the female who is mentioned as 'a wyf', 'womman', 'she', or by some other reference to the feminine, no less than twenty times. What does this suggest about the Parson's attitude towards women, do you think?

It certainly indicates a strong streak of anti-feminism. It seems that it is *woman* whose behaviour is most likely to be lustful or sinful, and *woman* whose behaviour requires careful control. At the same time, the types of conduct he recommends clearly privilege the male. The speaker of this sermon-tale notes that a wife should be subservient to her husband, and be 'subget' to he 'that is hire lorde'. She should be obedient to him; as a wife she has 'noon auctoritee' of her own and can do little 'withoute leve of hir housbonde'. She is instructed to 'serven hym', to 'plesen' him, to 'loven hire housbonde with al hire herte, and to hym be trewe of hir body', and also to worship him body and soul if she is to achieve a 'parfit mariage'. At the same time there is a long digression, carefully supported by those other anti-feminist authorities Jerome and Gregory, concerning female dress. Women are advised that ostentatious clothing, fancy silks and strong colours, are unsuitable. Instead they ought to 'been attempree' (modest) in their choice of what to wear. To do otherwise is to indicate vanity. The Parson warns that external beauty coupled with inner lack or ugliness is 'a greet folye', subtly managing to imply that woman's intrinsic nature is inclined to be 'foul' rather than 'fair'. To compensate, she should work hard to ensure that her appearance and her behaviour is both modest and discreet.

The Parson briefly touches on the institution of marriage in this extract where, once again, his bald remarks are revealing. They indicate that this cleric's views are firmly entrenched and offered as an ideal or gold standard by which everyone ought to live their lives. A husband too, he argues, should love his wife body and soul but, just in case anyone interprets this as licence for sexual delight even in wedlock, he reminds us that man and woman are joined together for three things. The main thing is to produce children 'to the service of God'. Another is to avoid sin including lechery, and the third concerns the issue of conjugal rights where each must yield 'the dette of hire bodies, for neither of hem hath power of his owene body'. What is missing, of course, is any indication of joy in sexuality, or sexual union as a physical expression of love.

This then is the ideal, known to all, by which medieval men and women were to live their lives. It is presented to us here in a straightforward serious manner, a demand and not a discussion, its apparent lack of irony making it all the more horrifying to many contemporary sensibilities. There appears to be none of what you are probably expecting from Chaucer by now – ambiguity, contradiction, subtlety – yet both its speaker and its very place in the *Tales* alert us to other possibilities and viewpoints we have already seen expressed elsewhere. If you re-read any of the tales discussed so far, how might this extract clarify or even contradict your earlier opinions?

It is perhaps a fitting note on which to introduce our final extract, another piece offered as 'authority' concerning the relationship between the sexes, this time spoken by a woman who is certainly not moderate in her behaviour or modest in her dress – the Wife of Bath. Her words set the tone for what she is about to tell us but what light do they shed upon Chaucer's continuing concern with these ideas?

> "Experience, though noon auctoritee
> Were in this world, is right ynogh for me
> To speke of wo that is in mariage;
> For, lordynges, sith that I twelve yeer was of age,
> Thonked be God that is eterne on lyve,
> Housbondes at chirche dore I have had fyve –
> If I so ofte myghte have ywedded bee –
> And alle were worthy men in hir degree.
> But me was toold, certeyn, nat longe agoon is,
> That sith that Crist ne wente nevere but onis
> To weddyng, in the Cane of Galilee,
> That by the same ensample taughte he me
> That I ne sholde wedded be but ones.
> Herkne eek, lo, which a sharp word for the / nones,
> Biside a welle, Jhesus, God and man,
> Spak in repreeve of the Samaritan:
> 'Thou hast yhad fyve housbondes,' quod he,
> 'And that ilke man that now hath thee
> Is noght thyn housbonde,' thus seyde he cer-/teyn.
> What that he mente therby, I kan nat seyn;
> But that I axe, why that the fifthe man
> Was noon housbonde to the Samaritan?
> How manye myghte she have in mariage?
> Yet herde I nevere tellen in myn age
> Upon this nombre diffinicioun.
> Men may devyne and glosen, up and doun,
> But wel I woot, expres, withoute lye,
> God bad us for to wexe and multiplye;
> That gentil text kan I wel understonde.
> Eek wel I woot, he seyde myn housbonde
> Sholde lete fader and mooder and take to me.
> But of no nombre mencion made he,
> Of bigamye, or of octogamye;
> Why sholde men thanne speke of it vileynye?
>
> (III (D), ll.1–34)

The Wife's opening line introduces a division between 'Experience' and 'auctoritee' that is continued throughout the rest of the passage. She offers details of her own life, that she was first married at twelve years old and that she has had five husbands, implying that this has allowed her to form a set of personal beliefs about marriage. She then sets this belief against what she knows of 'That gentil text', interpreted for her by men who 'devyne and glosen' an authoritative and definitive version of events giving rise to a standard of ideal behaviour.

Let us examine what she says as well as *how* she says it. She speaks of 'the same ensaumple' of Christ's attendance at a wedding in Galilee, and of His words to the Samaritan. Alison's focus is upon specific examples taken from the Bible as evidence supposedly supporting clerical teaching and Church rules governing behaviour. In this way a generalisation is 'glosen' from a particular example. What Alison does, however, is to invert the process.

First, she offers her own examples and draws inferences from them. Secondly, she makes her 'teaching' intensely personal. Thus it is the individual that is emphasised, something seen in the way she shows how teaching affects people, particularly through the language chosen to describe it. Alison uses phrases such as 'for me', 'I have had', 'I axe', 'herde I nevere tellen in myn age', 'wel I woot', and 'I wel understonde'. In addition there are things like 'me was toold', 'quod he', 'thus seyde he cer-/teyn', 'he mente', or 'men thanne speke of it'.

The Wife's opening declaration is entirely unambiguous; she places *her* trust in 'Experience' when it comes to any comment concerning the 'wo that is in mariage', and this experience is a personal one. The start of line four offers her credentials. She thinks that she is able to pronounce with some authority on this subject for she herself has been married since she was twelve and 'housbondes at chirche dore I have had fyve'. This, by implication, excludes any other men with whom she might have dallied.

Her next remark draws attention to the authoritative pronouncement of the Church which is opposed to her own lived experience. Alison has been 'toold' that she should only have married once, that she should have taken as her example the 'fact' that Christ attended only one wedding in the Bible. This written authority offers her an 'ensample' by which she should have been 'taughte'. Yet the same biblical text is open to interpretation as the Wife suggests when she instructs her listeners to 'Herkne', and relates the occasion of Christ telling the Samaritan that since she had wed five husbands

> 'that ilke man that now hath thee
> Is noght thyn housbonde'.

However, far from offering this as final proof of a proscription against remarriage, the Wife questions its authority.

She remarks 'What that he mente therby, I kan nat seyn', a comment that underscores not her implied ignorance but the ambiguity of such examples and their openness to interpretation. She asks why the fifth husband is not a legitimate one and how many the woman might be permitted to marry, concluding that she has never, in all her life, heard anyone tell 'Upon this nombre diffinicioun'. It is not the specific answers to these questions that is important but the very fact that Alison is prepared to ask them; they remain a crucial part of Chaucer's attempt to use the Wife as a vehicle for indicating the slippery nature of so-called fixed authority. Alison's comments are, of course, only one personal opinion as exemplified by the repetition of 'I' in 'I kan nat seyn', 'I axe', 'herde I nevere tellen' and so on, but, nevertheless, her perspective *is* an alternative, that of lived 'Experience'.

The theme is expanded as the Wife continues to question this particular and apparently definitive aspect of Christ's teaching. She states that 'Men may devyne and glosen, up and doun', highlighting the fact that such authoritative interpretations of the Bible, or of any other written texts, are male-dominated. But, she implies, theirs is only one opinion amongst many, for *her* understanding is different. Alison offers an alternative piece of biblical evidence as contradiction, claiming

> 'But wel I woot, expres, withoute lye
> God bad us for to wexe and multiplye'.

At the same time 'Eek wel I woot, he seyde myn housbonde' should leave his parents and 'take to me'; there was no mention of how many times this might occur. Nor did Christ speak of bigamy or even marrying eight times, according to Alison.

Her understanding of biblical teaching may well be limited or partial. However, her very questioning of the masculine activity of exegetical authority – where those in religious office treat the Bible as an allegorical work awaiting man's search for its hidden 'sentence' (the fruit and not the chaff, as the Nun's Priest expressed it) so that its meaning is defined and fixed – is an extremely subversive act. Women were certainly not allowed to participate in the process while ordinary people of either sex were denied access to this making of meaning. They were required instead to try and live their lives according to an ideal pronounced by someone else. Alison dares to speak as a woman *and* offers her own lived experience as an alternative to this authority.

She concludes with a simple question, 'Why sholde men thanne speke of it vileynye?', but its abrupt frankness resonates with a deeper challenge. In effect she is saying that she too, an ignorant woman, has her own opinions formed by listening to others but also on the basis of practical day-to-day experience. Alison demands to know why her perspective is any less powerful or 'right' than any other, and in this way Chaucer offers his own challenge to notions of received authority as well as to the belief that the written word remained fixed as 'truth'.

Unlike the Wife, Chaucer is probably not asserting that 'Experience' rather than authority is the definitive way. Instead he leaves open the entire question, returning to it time and time again in a whole host of poems and in a manner perhaps entirely appropriate to the fact that this passage is the final one in both this chapter and in the series of chapters focusing primarily upon exploration of the text.

Before moving on to the *Further Reading* section, there are two other factors to consider at this point. First, read the rest of the *Prologue*, concentrating in particular upon moments when the Wife speaks of authority. How trustworthy is she as a fictional voice? Secondly, you could focus on a more general question, one which relates to a previous chapter, and that is in what way does the multiplicity of voice and narration, Chaucer's continual and slippery juxtaposition of events, ideas, and styles, contribute towards a dissolving of notions of writing as fixed authority?

Conclusion

This chapter has opened up consideration of a range of larger themes or interests in *The Canterbury Tales*. Though the list is far from being exhaustive it includes issues such as love and relationships between men and women, attitudes towards women, the role of the Church and the question of religious faith or belief, notions of social order and structure within its different social groups, plus wider issues such as feudal honour and chivalry or the influence of the commercial urban world, as well as notions of received authority and learning. Once again these ideas have been explored through close textual analysis with a focus upon one or more of the following:

1. word choice, especially the search for patterns and clusters which might be revealing
2. style: Is it high? Logical and reasoned? Comic? Literary? Action-packed?
3. structure: Is it disjointed or snapshot? Carefully linked via reasoned statements and semi-colons?
4. contrast and juxtaposition
5. rhythm, line breaks, pauses, punctuation
6. context of the tale: Who is its speaker? Is there any relation between the speaker and the tale? How does the tale fit into the overall structure of the *Tales*? What type of tale is told – fairy? realistic? non-realistic? fabliau?

Yet again Chaucer has proved to be a slippery writer who heaps ambiguity upon ambiguity. Often the issues he raises indicate a gap between a proposed and apparently fixed ideal and the reality of its practice. It seems that nothing is conclusive in Chaucer. He continually opens up questions and explores them via a multiplicity of tales, forms and voices. Is he reflecting the tensions and concerns of his time, do you think, or is he critical of those issues and realities?

Part 2 of this book focuses on Chaucer's world and also on some critics' views of his work whereas this section of the book has primarily offered my interpretation of Chaucer's poetry. It is important to be aware of the critics' perspectives but always remember it is *your informed opinion* that counts. The last few chapters have attempted to show you how to focus upon the text, how to form ideas and to substantiate them so that you are in a position to evaluate the comments of others, how to make judgements about the text and perhaps above all to identify the concerns as well as the limitations of the authorial voice.

Further Reading

Many of the themes and issues identified in this chapter are so closely interwoven that any attempt to concentrate on one to the exclusion of others can reduce the complexity of a particular tale. Once again, therefore, the following suggestions are designed for ease of reference rather than an attempt to define the individual poem.

If your interest is in love, women or sexual relationships you might care to explore the *Merchant's Tale*, the *Shipman's*, the *Franklin's*, the *Man of Law's*, the *Clerk's*, the *Knight's*, or the *Reeve's Tale*. The *Parson's Tale* also contains a section on the ideal of orthodox marriage. Similarly, saintly women are presented as ideals in the tales of the *Clerk*, the *Man of Law*, and the *Second Nun*.

The role of the Church is a predominant theme of the *Friar's Tale*, the *Summoner's*, the tale of the *Prioress*, the *Monk's*, and the *Parson's*. Chaucer's interest in the wider social world is demonstrated by the portraits in the *General Prologue*, and the tales of the *Knight*, the *Franklin*, the *Shipman*, the *Clerk*, and the *Squire*.

If you wish to explore the issue of knowledge, or the gap between authority and experience found in so many snippets of the *Tales* as a whole, then you might like to read the *Parson's Tale*, the *Nun's Priest's*, *Melibee's*, or the *Canon Yeoman's Tale*.

PART 2

THE CONTEXT AND THE CRITICS

5

Chaucer and His Work

I: CHAUCER'S LIFE AND WORKS

Chaucer was writing at the same time as authors like Gower, Lydgate and Langland. He was a writer held in esteem by his contemporaries and has frequently been described as the 'father of English literature'. One of the reasons behind this comment is undoubtedly the fact of Chaucer's contribution to a tradition of writing in English. Though not the first to use the ordinary and everyday or the mother-tongue in his writing, Chaucer was the first English poet to demonstrate the flexibility of his own language and to elevate it as a serious medium in an era when the language of the court and of officialdom was still French, and when Latin continued to be regarded as high and learned.

Records of Chaucer's life establish him as well-travelled, successful, hardworking, trusted by royalty, and connected to the influential of the land. He not only survived a difficult political period, which saw three different kings in his lifetime, but seems to have been closely linked with those royal courts where his varied and numerous responsibilities brought him into contact with a great variety of people both at home and abroad.

Chaucer was a soldier, civil servant and court poet. The exact date and place of his birth is unknown but it seems likely that sometime between 1340 and 1344 he was born into a well-to-do family of London vintners or wine merchants. His parents had property in Vintry Ward, one of the two wealthiest areas of medieval London.

Records suggest that this was a cosmopolitan enclave with Gascon wine merchants and Italian and Flemish families all living there. Around 1357, as a young boy, Chaucer entered the household of the Countess of Ulster, wife of Prince Lionel who was King Edward III's third son. We think that Chaucer was probably a page, and from there it appears that he accompanied the prince on a military campaign to France where, as a young man, he was captured and briefly held before the king ransomed him in 1359 or 1360. Evidence indicates that later in that year Chaucer was paid to carry letters home to England, the first of many journeys as trusted ambassador or envoy. A gap in remaining records leaves a six-year period of silence.

By the mid-1360s, however, Chaucer's career as a valued retainer was established. During the period 1367–86, he remained closely allied to the court of Edward III. By now he was also married to a lady named Philippa, herself in service to Edward's queen and part of a family enjoying royal privilege. In 1367 Chaucer was rewarded with a royal annuity and was possibly also studying among lawyers at the Inns of Court. His journeys abroad continued. Four trips to France are recorded for the latter half of the 1360s, and later travels on the king's business appear to have taken him to Genoa and Florence. Chaucer's web of influential connections spread too when he and his wife gained additional annuities from the powerful John of Gaunt, Edward's fourth son. John of Gaunt was also the lover, and later husband, of Philippa's sister Katherine Swynford.

At the same time, Chaucer extended his work as a civil servant. After 1374, when it seems he was no longer living with his wife, he gained the important post of customs house controller overseeing the vital exports of wool and later taking additional control of petty customs, collecting duties on such things as wine. He spent twelve years there, longer that anyone else, but towards the end of this period he made increasing use of deputies to cover his duties, while he continued to make trips to France and Italy (1377–8) acting as the king's envoy. At the same time Chaucer also removed himself from London and established himself in Kent where he became a JP and, later, an MP in 1386.

The late 1380s marks a quieter period in Chaucer's life. 1387 is the last recorded foreign embassy for some time, though the years themselves involved some political upheaval. By 1389, when Richard II had ascended to the throne, Chaucer's continuing and circumspect loyalty was rewarded with a position as Clerk of the King's Works, followed by the even more influential and well-paid post as sub-forester at the royal forest of Petherton Park in 1391. He also received an annuity from Richard which was doubled on the day of the subsequent king's coronation. In 1394 Chaucer took up a fifty-three-year lease on a house in Westminster but then died at the close of the century in 1400.

We retain many details of Chaucer's life and career considering his time; undoubtedly much of this information has come via the records of his own office and official duties. The picture they present of the man is more difficult to judge, but what is clear is that here was a worldly fellow, well-travelled, educated, speaking several languages, a trusted ambassador relied upon and rewarded by no fewer than three kings as well as some of the most influential men of his day; diplomatic, loyal and circumspect, there exists little evidence to tarnish his reputation.

It is astonishing to think that throughout this demanding time Chaucer was writing continually. His literary output was considerable especially in view of the fact that some works are lost to us. What is believed to be his first completed work classifies him as a court poet and directly links him with what was probably the most influential family of his time. In the service and payment of the royal household, including that of John of Gaunt, Chaucer's *Book of the Duchess* (1368–9) is generally assumed to be an elegy for Blanche, Duchess of Lancaster, Gaunt's first wife. Thus Chaucer's early writing is in response to the demands of his patron. Though entirely in keeping with the literary traditions of the time, this had far-reaching effects upon his literary career.

Chaucer's output increased dramatically during the 1370s, beginning with shorter, smaller works and moving on to longer pieces. This is the decade during which he was controlling customs' operations and undertaking ambassadorial duties in France and Italy. He was increasingly in contact with a world beyond the court, with other collectors and merchants, and with other royal households and officials. At the same time too, he might well have been made aware of new literary influences. It is perhaps no surprise that 1370 saw his partial translation from the French of the influential *Le Roman de la Rose*, while his travels to Italy might have brought him into contact, if not with the authors themselves (the former were still alive), then with the important works of Petrarch, Boccaccio and Dante. As his influences broadened, his work began to reflect a wider range of styles and sources, as well as demonstrating the stirrings of an artistic command that took him beyond simple love-visions to the development of the role of the narrator, a device enabling Chaucer to undercut surface narratives and open up his poetry to a range of interpretations. The period 1372–80 saw him working on individual tales like the *Second Nun's* and the *Monk's* (both later part of *The Canterbury Tales*), the courtly love poem *Anelida and Arcite*, followed by the incomplete *House of Fame*, and *The Parliament of Fowls*.

During the 1380s Chaucer moved away from London and the courtly circle to Kent, though he remained bound by their sphere of influence as an MP. This was a time of political upheaval with the Peasants' Revolt in 1381 and, in later years, the power struggles of Richard II. Chaucer's literary output increased during this period and at the same time his writings became increasingly complex, a reflection perhaps of the social tensions of this decade. During the early 1380s Chaucer wrote what later became the *Knight's*, the *Parson's*, the *Man of Law's*, the *Physician's*, and the *Manciple's* tales in *The Canterbury Tales*, even though this last lengthy poem had not yet materialised as a coherent whole. He also translated Boethius's *Consolation of Philosophy – Boece*.

The influence of this work is discussed in the next chapter, but this was clearly the beginning of a structure of ideas, and of the formulation of a vision where Fortune is set against the notion of free will, a theme crucial to the major work of this period in Chaucer's life, *Troilus and Criseyde*. The '*Troilus*' poem is also concerned with love and its failures, as well as the demands and expectations of gender roles, and perhaps sees the pinnacle of Chaucer's use of a dreamy, unreliable narrator, the courtly poet, who is set the task of concocting from earlier sources of this story a tale of love enacted against the backdrop of the Greek–Trojan war. This narrator must rework earlier versions to satisfy some kind of 'truth' or authority, and to satisfy the demands of a sophisticated audience, yet finds himself struggling to reconcile all this. The tale slips and slides away from him, and so opens up the whole question of how to write, how to tell a tale – issues raised in earlier poems such as the *House of Fame* and *The Parliament of Fowls* with their dreaming narrators, and taken up again in the mid 1380s in Chaucer's next major achievement, *The Legend of Good Women.*

The *Legend* is a poem which focuses very clearly upon the act of writing. The narrator of this work is instructed by his female patron to write a book in defence of Criseyde, in defence of all women, to portray them as good and virtuous for once instead of in classic anti-feminist mode. As the poem progresses, the narrator is unable to comply with the request, becoming more and more concerned with the heroic and martial exploits of the male protagonists, adopting a gallant guise that fails to meet the requirements of his commission until eventually his story fades away. Here Chaucer fully realises the narrator as ironic mask or *persona* begun so much earlier in his work, and possibly developed in response to new continental literary influences or an increasingly tense and dissatisfied age. As a court poet he continued to focus upon the courtly love-visions demanded by his audience, yet we also see signs that his talent as an author was developing. We can see in his more mature work a concern to push back the boundaries of writing. Possibly this is why Chaucer's public life is a little quieter during this time, or why he felt it necessary to remove himself from London and its royal circles for a while.

The culmination of this is *The Canterbury Tales,* a huge but fragmentary and unfinished collection of tales begun in 1386 and ongoing even at the time of the author's death. Here Chaucer fully develops the notion of a series of conflicting or unreliable narratorial voices, utilises a diversity of genres undoubtedly discovered throughout his studies and travels at home and abroad, and realises the vision begun in the two poems mentioned above of opening up narrative, of stimulating a multiplicity of perspective. Interestingly this mature work seems to move away from courtly love themes, and instead is centred upon a wider spectrum of ideas in response to the social tensions and upheavals of the day; it demonstrates a concern with the notion of writing itself, hence its use of different types or genres of story. The *Tales* works to exhibit Chaucer's expertise in writing all sorts of stories, but at the same time challenges us and forces us to reconsider many of our expectations of storytelling. Chaucer worked on the *Tales* until his death.

From 1391 onwards Chaucer began to be drawn back into London life, resuming his duties as a civil servant. It is perhaps no surprise that his final works are minor poems, adjuncts to his real concern, the *Tales*, and possibly even responses to the need to earn a living and satisfy his patrons. These poems, *A Treatise on the Astrolabe*, *Equatories of the Planets*, and a series of short works such as *A Compleynt of Chaucer unto his Purse*, are not generally regarded as influential pieces.

II: THEMES AND CONCERNS IN CHAUCER'S WORK

What then are the major concerns of Chaucer's writings? The first is undoubtedly narrative art itself but it might be useful to begin with a consideration of some of the influences upon his work.

Travel to France and Italy certainly brought him into contact with some highly influential authors and their stories. These included the Italians – Dante, Petrarch and Boccaccio – as well as the French courtly love poets, and possibly even the writings of Frenchwomen like Marie de France with her Breton *lais* (fairy or folk tales), and Christine de Pisan. Also influential, and discussed in the next chapter, was the famous medieval poem *Le Roman de la Rose*, both Guillaume de Lorris's early version and Jean de Meun's later reworking of it.

These continental influences led to several things. One is the way in which Chaucer chose to write. Not only did his ideas take poetic form, but they made use of one or more narrators, and of courtly dream visions, especially in earlier works such as the dream-like *Book of the Duchess*, or the dreamers in the *House of Fame* and *The Parliament of Fowls*. Another aspect concerns the sorts of stories with which Chaucer must have come into contact, a huge variety of tales told and retold, written and rewritten – saints' lives, folk tales, romances, epic exploits, fable, *fabliaux* or carnivalesque-grotesque, dream or love visions, or the actual story-collection genre itself. Such influences gave rise to the *Second Nun's Tale*, the *Clerk's Tale* of Patient Griselda, the *Man of Law's* or *Sir Thopas*, the *Knight's*, or the *Miller's* respectively (all in the *Tales*), or else the *Book of the Duchess's* dream, the love-debates of *The Parliament of Fowls* and the *Romance of the Rose*, and of course *The Canterbury Tales* itself. In addition, we see the use of sermon or didactic stories in the *Parson's Tale* or *Melibee's*, while earlier Anglo-Saxon alliterative poems give us *Sir Thopas* and are reflected in the folk-romance styles of the *Clerk's* or the *Man of Law's*. Similarly, Chaucer, like all authors of the time, took as his source or inspiration the writings of Roman poets like Ovid from whom he borrowed for *The Legend of Good Women*. (The rewriting and retelling of earlier tales was not regarded as copying or seen to be lacking in originality.) What perhaps makes Chaucer unique is his mingling of these diverse influences, tales from home and abroad, past and present, in French, Italian, Latin and English.

Without doubt, though, Chaucer's main interest was in the art of writing. His work reflects his quest to marry original sources with his own ideas, questions notions of how tales are told, plays with and pushes to the limits the conventions of writing so that boundaries are altered, perceived ideas challenged, the expectations of listeners and readers fractured, and perspectives opened up. His writings exhibit the development of his narrative art, starting with the naive narrators of his early work, and moving to narrator-as-ironic-mask, seen in many of our extracts in Part 1, a narration that disturbs, undercuts and poses questions which frequently remain unanswered. The second major question, then, is what does Chaucer write about?

To begin with his focus is upon the theme of love, as expected by his courtly audience, and seen in the *Book of the Duchess*, *Romance of the Rose*, *Anelida and Arcite*, the *Knight's Tale*, or the love debate of *The Parliament of Fowls*. Yet the influence of de Meun's version of the *Rose* meant that this type of poetry had already undergone a change. Increasingly it became a device for making political statements, questioning feudal order, mocking or challenging social constructs. Such ideas may well have been prevalent in Chaucer's first works; certainly *The Parliament of Fowls* is only a love debate on the surface, the three courtly eagles fighting for the favours of their one lady, intimating of feudal order, notions of chivalry, love and art. Similarly in the *House of Fame*, the dreamer who contemplates the walls of Venus's temple, upon which is depicted the love story of the betrayed Dido, before being taken by the eagle to learn of the love tidings that will provide material for his poetry, also centres upon the art of narrative itself. By the time Chaucer was writing *The Legend of Good Women* and *Troilus and Criseyde*, the theme of love was inextricably linked to a mix of ideas gathered together by an untrustworthy narrator to provide material for an extremely complicated poem. Through this same line of development the concept of feudal order can also be traced, beginning with a challenge to its probably outdated ideal in the *Knight's Tale*.

Much of Chaucer's writing is also informed by his knowledge of Boethian philosophy. Midway through his literary career, he translated *The Consolation of Philosophy* written by the Roman author Boethius and heavily influenced by Greek scholarship. Written as a dialogue between an imprisoned man and his 'muse' Philosophy, whose instruction restores him to health and brings him spiritual enlightenment, the poem depicts the search for what is true and good as opposed to the false vanity of worldly or temporal things. Order stems from divine Providence, evil and suffering have a purpose, and all is stabilized by 'charitas' or an unselfish, benevolent, higher love. Life is governed by this and by man's free will which, if he chooses to exercise it, can bring enlightenment. This clash between fate or fortune and free will is a theme of *Troilus and Criseyde* in particular.

It is possible, therefore, for us to begin the process of identifying those tensions, challenges and ambivalences for which Chaucer is famed. Notions of courtly love and feudal order or chivalry begin to be outdated by the late Middle Ages, and to undergo a change. They are replaced by other concerns which are reflected in Chaucer's writing. By the time Chaucer arrives at the *Tales*, his focus is increasingly upon the prevalence of commercial or material interests (see the *Shipman's Tale* or the *Wife of Bath's Prologue*), and the effects such unsettling tensions have on ordinary people from all walks of life. The power of the Church is examined and dissected too. Chaucer explores and criticises its internal wranglings, its political and economic strength, and its stifling sphere of influence over the way people lived their lives (see the *Wife of Bath's Prologue*, the *Pardoner's Tale*, the *Merchant's Tale*).

What finally remains is Chaucer's overriding concern with that gap between the ideal and practice, between authority and experience, that problematical ambivalence arising from the way Church, political system and government, plus textual and written authority combined to tell people how they *should* behave, in contrast to the way medieval people actually made sense of their lives, or discovered how to circumvent the near-impossibility of those ideals. Chaucer's writing opens up this gap through his attempts to shape and order his narrative, through the development of a series of complex, sometimes ironic, narratorial voices, and through his own refusal as a writer to simply accept that versions of tales written long before his stand as final, definitive, authoritative accounts.

6

The Context of Chaucer's Works

We began our discussion of the literary context of Chaucer's writing in the previous chapter, where we particularly noticed the influences of a host of continental authors, earlier Greek and Roman writers, such as Boethius, Ovid, Virgil and, more generally, Chaucer's abiding interest in all forms of narrative. His choice of English as the language of his texts sees the start of a move away from traditional notions of Latin as learned or French as the official language, as opposed to the popular but somehow inferior writing of the vernacular, the language of the ordinary. Similarly, Chaucer elevated a different style of verse form, away from the alliterative tradition of Anglo-Saxon, parodied in the tale of *Sir Thopas*, to something more flexible and sophisticated, adapted from French and Italian cultures. Our discussion noted too how early influences of French writers like Machaut and Froissart led to Chaucer's interest in love visions and love debates, later developed through the inspiration of the highly influential *Le Roman de la Rose*.

Why was this work considered so important? It is a thirteenth-century allegorical poem centred upon a young man who dreams he is in a beautiful garden where he meets a variety of characters personifying feudal values or virtues, and where love is the main preoccupation. Originally written by Guillaume de Lorris, this allegory of courtly love dominated literary circles until it was rewritten forty years later by Jean de Meun. In de Meun's version, it became an intellectual satire of the contemporary world. The dominant character in his poem is False-Seeming who presides over a corrupt, deceitful and self-seeking world. Other important figures are Reason and Nature. What is significant about this version is its pervasive influence and its effect upon style and theme with its mixture of ironic humour and serious comment.

Chaucer's influences were not solely literary, however. Quite possibly, his development as an artist was partly affected by his own unique social standing. Chaucer was attached to the royal court and its prestigious and powerful circles through a family network, through his employment, and also in his role as a writer in which he was obliged to satisfy the demands of an audience largely socially superior to him and who required tales of love. To complicate matters, an entire literary tradition expected a poet to entertain, but also to instruct and offer some form of moral conclusion. The court poet of fourteenth-century England was a marginalised figure, unable to offend his social 'betters' and his patrons, those people calling the tune. Since Chaucer's career as a court official or civil servant was apparently unaffected by his role as court poet, neither prompting advancement nor holding it back, we might reasonably assume that the two remained largely separate, possibly enabling some detachment in terms of ideas, and permitting other influences, perhaps that awareness of the commercial world mentioned in the previous chapter.

Finally, there is the self-effacing narrator of so many of Chaucer's texts, possibly a partial product of his own difficult social position, and certainly a creation designed to prompt ambiguity, a fracturing of surface narrative, and an exploration of tensions and ambivalences begun in the groundbreaking version of the courtly love poem by de Meun.

Chaucer's works must also be seen in the context of an era which saw many changes concerning the reception of texts, with inevitable consequences for their writing since author and audience were bound together in their production. In an age when most people remained illiterate and uneducated, a literary audience would have been an aural one. Tales would have been related verbally, and told with all the effects that oral transmission has upon the changing shape of stories – the content that shifts in the retelling, the addresses and exhortations to the listener, rhetorical devices to maintain interest and signify breaks between sub-plot and main narrative, and the tags to draw attention to certain areas or highlight the moral in a didactic tale. Audiences would have been familiar with a wide variety of tales in diverse form: sermons, fables, folk-lore or fairy-tales, beast fables, biblical stories, *exempla* or little stories forming part of Church teaching, saints' lives and so on.

Yet the late medieval period was also the dawn of literacy. The advent of the printing press in the fourteenth century meant that stories were collected, compiled, commissioned and widely circulated. For the first time literature was not restricted to an exchange between an educated, elitist and closed set of communities, namely monasteries and convents. The printed word was beginning to be passed between countries and to reach a wider audience, both literate, and those simply listening to stories. Those unable to write but with a story to tell found an amanuensis to act as their scribe, or simply allowed their stories to be told by others.[1] Books like Jacobus de Voragine's *Legenda Aurea*, which began life as a collection of age-old saints' lives and other biblical or Greco-Roman tales of Christians outwitting paganism, was translated from the Latin, and then into a variety of other languages including French, and later English. Such was its popularity that it was reprinted many times, but it remains one example amongst many as compilers and printers like William Caxton, and the later Wynkyn de Worde, increased in prominence.

Women were especially renowned as book collectors, inspired perhaps by the example of Richard's queen, Anne, who brought her own library with her from France and added to it in England. All kinds of things were collected, not just poems or stories. *Books of Hours* or *Days* were designed to instruct in the Christian faith, and to aid in the keeping of the liturgical calendar as well as daily religious rites, but they also included popular stories, short fables or romances. Collected mainly by women, these books were passed on to sons and daughters. Both men and women began to commission works extending the net of patronage beyond the court, whilst more generally, manuscripts continued to be written and compiled in religious institutions, and official records, including wills, were retained as usual.

Chaucer's audience is generally assumed to have been a courtly and sophisticated one, composed of many different types of people including the aristocratic as well as a more bourgeois class, and comprising both sexes. Straddling two literary cultures, an oral and a printed one, Chaucer's writings, like others of the period, reflect both. They retain an oral transmission quality. We see this in the use of a narrator to move stories on, in a series of digressions, asides or comments to the audience, and also in an acknowledgement and awareness of those who might have commissioned works in the first place. Very often a self-effacing narrator declares himself unworthy of his task, and tells us that he is obliged to fulfil the remit given to him by his patron. Thus Chaucer juggles both written and oral sources as seen in poems like *Troilus and Criseyde* or *The Legend of Good Women*, responds to his patron in *The Legend of Good Women* again or his real life one in the *Book of the Duchess*, and invents an *oral* storytelling contest as a framing device for *The Canterbury Tales*.

If the literary context of Chaucer's writing was a rich and varied one, the historical context was no less dramatic. It was a time of political upheaval with three successive kings. Moreover, two of these monarchs assumed the throne only after a great deal of difficulty. Richard II followed Edward III's reign, one which saw continued war with France. Amidst a great power struggle, he finally ascended to the throne despite much faction-making, rivalry, and some unpopularity. His French wife, Anne, ensured that his court retained some literary and cultural influence, but it was essentially feudal with French being the official language. The year of 1397 was one of great unrest, with Richard arresting his enemies, killing, imprisoning, and exiling many, including Henry, son of John of Gaunt, a man who had enjoyed great power and prestige under Edward. When John of Gaunt died in 1399, Richard seized his estates. Henry returned from exile to reclaim them, and deposed Richard in order to become King Henry IV himself.

This unrest also manifested itself in social upheaval. Many soldiers, retainers, and mercenaries were left penniless, sometimes homeless, after an uneasy truce with France, and were forced to beg or become vagrants. In 1381 thousands of common people and workers entered London in protest against taxation, burning the palace of John of Gaunt and beheading the archbishop of Canterbury, in what became known as the Peasants' Revolt. The late medieval period witnessed a tremendous population growth in the towns and cities with all the attendant problems, as people moved from agricultural work, lured by the usually false prospect of a better life. Life was hard, often violent. The infant mortality rate was high, life expectancy short for the vast majority of people, (around 30?), and disease rife due to overcrowding, poor sanitation, and ignorance, as well as several outbreaks of the plague.

What is perhaps forgotten, though, is that this was also a time of cultural advance, not the Dark Ages so commonly depicted. It saw advances in literature and literacy, the invention of the printing press, the establishment of libraries and book collections. It gave us a legacy of art and artistic treasures, great pieces of architecture with cathedrals and churches. It witnessed advances in scientific knowledge and learning, fostered a spirit of charity with its pilgrimages and hospital work, and laid an economic foundation with trade in wool and textiles, and the establishment of guilds and craft corporations.

The social tensions explored in Chaucer's work undoubtedly existed, however. Initially society was dominated by the notion of feudal order where all unquestioningly accepted their place or 'estate', offered allegiance to the nobility and ultimately to the king, who was commonly believed to be an intermediary between God and humankind. The emergence of a profit economy, allied to urban development, placed great strain upon this concept of order, a theme particularly reflected in *The Canterbury Tales*. Notions of 'gentillesse', with its emphasis on the privilege of birth, and upon unbroken promises or 'trouthe', are questioned in the *Franklin's* and the *Wife's* tales for example, and also explored in *The Parliament of Fowls*. In practice it seems highly unlikely that the feudal order held, especially as wealth, prestige and privilege began to be claimed by those who had worked and made money, or acquired possessions via their own commercial acumen rather than having claimed it as their birthright.

Of especial importance was the power and influence of the medieval Church which pervaded every sphere of life. It set itself up as the only medium of God's grace, insisting that there was no salvation outside its formidable institution or clerical apparatus. The Church pronounced authoritatively on everything, on the nature of God and the universe, as might be expected, but also on the way people lived by prescribing personal behaviour. It established rules by which the Bible and other religious texts were to be interpreted, setting itself up as literary authority too. At the same time, its power was male-dominated, and inextricably bound up with that of the ruling classes, involving itself in law-making, papal courts, civic and ecclesiastical legislation, the collection of fees or 'taxes' for the carrying out of various functions, and the admonishment of sins. Inevitably it controlled all aspects of preaching, including the pardoning of sins via the sale of 'indulgences' or praying for souls in purgatory. All clerics, but especially friars, were issued with instructions on how to read and interpret the Bible. Biblical texts were viewed as allegorical and so ordinary people supposedly required explanations of meaning which only the Church could provide. This process of clerical interpretation was known as 'glosyng'. An entire apparatus – of confession, of penance, preaching, 'glosyng', even pilgrimage – might be said to have been based upon economic considerations with corruption rife even amongst those in church office.

Thus the institution of the medieval Church spread its authoritative influence politically, economically and socially. It remained highly involved in secular affairs, a prime example being its rules governing the function and enactment of marriage. The Church taught that marriage was solely for the procreation of children, who should be then raised in the ways of Catholicism. Marriage was also said to control 'incontinence' or lust, and was a means of focusing the sex drive in order to avoid fornication and adultery. It preached that the enjoyment of sex was sinful, even within marriage, and that the act was purely to engender children or for the 'payment' of what was described as the marital 'dette', whereby the wife in particular had a conjugal duty to submit to the sexual demands of her husband. Such views were entirely rooted in a deep-seated and pervasive anti-feminism, and specifically neglected the notion of love or enjoyment, indeed categorically warned against the dangers of physical pleasure.

This socio-economic basis of marriage was, of course, entirely in keeping with a social purpose. Many marriages were arranged and people united on the basis of money, lands, and property. Such unions were designed to ensure the provision of (male) heirs in a patriarchal society. Church teaching, social taboo and secular legislation combined to outlaw incest, for example, while adultery was regarded as an offence, not against the person or as an act of disloyalty, but against male property rights.[2] Nevertheless, though, many people married for love.

The male was always dominant, supported by the Church and its teachings. Women were required to be obedient, compliant and even silent, for there was a profound fear of what was viewed as their potentially voracious sexual appetite or disruptive chatter and gossip.[3] Public power was limited to men, yet in reality, in the day-to-day running of affairs, women assumed many of the responsibilities.

During periods of war or absence, aristocratic women would manage the estate while, more generally, they dealt with the often complex affairs of the household. Peasant women worked the land, and in the towns too they were regarded as part of the economic unit, paying half of any tax imposed. At the same time women were experts in a variety of crafts such as brewing, butchery, embroidery, gardening, book-selling, or money-lending. They worked as drapers, tavern keepers, in the pottery and textile industries, and were permitted female apprentices, but never allowed public exercise of their power.[4] Marriage appears to have been the big divide between men and women, with the latter surrendering all legal and civic rights, money, property and lands to the husband – unless they were widowed, when it all reverted back, a process which inevitably led to much pressure to remarry.

The late medieval Church was subject to some testing times despite its apparent stranglehold on the lives of ordinary men and women. As convents began to close their doors to all but the very rich, there was a corresponding rise in lay piety, especially female. Several important movements were formed, many of which were regarded as heretical for one reason or another. These included groups like the Poor Clares, which was intended as a parallel to the Franciscan ideal of mendicant poverty, but in practice forbidden to preach and enclosed within a convent order. An extremely important, though largely continental, influence was the proliferating number of beguines. These were communities of mainly women, but occasionally men, to whom individuals might be loosely attached or fully involved. Their vows were few and largely revolved around charitable acts. Members could remain married and were free to leave at any time. The beguine movement was heavily involved with hospital work, and with education, and was self-supporting, forming its own guilds. As such it was a threat to the economic as well as spiritual power of the established Church and eventually outlawed, disappearing altogether.

Many other so-called heretical movements presented a challenge to the medieval Church with their questioning of that institution's sole right to grant grace or salvation. In England the Lollards presented a problem for the existing Church with their insistence upon the fact that a cleric was not required to deliver the sacrament, for the cleric himself was not, they claimed, the medium of the Host's transformation or transubstantiation. This doctrine was a major blow to clerical power.

This lay piety is especially reflected in the canonisation of huge numbers of new saints during this time, and the rise of leading religious figures, women in particular. Women such as Catherine of Siena, Mary of Oignies, Elizabeth of Hungary, Julian of Norwich and Margery of Kempe followed on from a tradition earlier established by Christina of Markyate, Birgitta of Sweden, and Hildegard de Bingen. Notably, many religious women were married; there was a shift in the image of the virgin as the highest ideal whereby the notion of virginity became a psychological rather than a literal 'fact', in effect simply an agreement to remain chaste or pure in thought.[5]

It was the Church's response to these threats, its ability to accommodate them, as well as its own internal corruption and monetary greed that, along with a whole host of other social tensions, informed much of Chaucer's writing, allowing him to explore the gap between the ideals the Church promoted and the resistant practices of ordinary people who did not always obey the rules.

Without doubt, the historical map of Chaucer's era is changing all the time as new discoveries come to light and different approaches are adopted for the exploration of the period. Details such as those given here remain sketchy and, at times, controversial – an open mind is perhaps the best prerequisite of any reading of the history of this period. Additional information can be obtained from a wealth of books and other sources, and you would do well to examine some of them before moving on to the next section.

7

Critical Approaches to Chaucer's Work

This chapter is intended as a guide to approaching critical works as well as a sampling of some influential ideas concerning Chaucer's writing. You will notice that the approach used here is an open-ended one. There will be an outline of each critic's views and a more detailed examination of one or more textual commentaries, chosen to correspond to the poems cited in Part 1. Our intention is that you form your own ideas concerning the value of these critical perspectives. The following questions are designed to help you in this and might be worth keeping in mind as you read.

1. What is this critic's frame of reference or context for his or her argument? Is this approach openly declared or implicit in the language or terminology used? Does this perspective qualify this critic's ideas in any way, or affect your own stance?
2. Is the critical argument supported by reference to the text or its details? Can you test out the theories by looking at the same tale yourself? Does the argument still hold if you do the same with other tales or poems? Does it matter if it does not?
3. Are you convinced by this argument? If not, why not, and if yes, how? Is it the ideas and evidence that convince you (or not as the case may be), or is it a persuasive style of writing? Do you have a vested interest or prejudice yourself which closes your mind or possibly blinds you to other ideas?

The aim is to examine the views of four very different critical perspectives. The chosen critics are David Aers, Helen Cooper, Elaine Tuttle Hansen and Alfred David.

DAVID AERS[6]

A cursory examination of both the format of Aers's books and his terminology quickly offers some clues concerning his interests and likely critical approach. Chapter headings tend to centre upon themes such as the commercial and material world, political ideas like lordship and feudal order, or are divided into sections like Chaucer's representations of society, religion, marriage and sexual relationships. One chapter is headed 'Order and Ideology'. In another, 'Love, Sex, and Marriage', the nominated issues are placed into a social context as well as the literary tradition of the time to suggest how Chaucer might have engaged with anti-feminism.[7] A closer look at word choice will help you to confirm your first impressions of David Aers and his ideas. Aers likes to use words such as 'community', 'ideology', 'institution', 'individual', 'identity', 'consciousness', 'cultural systems', 'social practices', and 'reified'. In addition he states,

> For texts, immersed in history, are social acts. Through them the world is mediated, prevalent perceptions are reinforced or challenged, contemporary values, experiences and problems represented, worked over. They are, indeed, made by the actual people in living relationships, but made within determinate systems (social, political, linguistic, sexual, literary), and within circumstances they have not chosen. Any attempt to understand literature must include the attempt to re-place it in the web of discourses, social relations and practices where it was produced, the attempt to discover what problems, what questions it was addressing. (Aers, 1986: 23)

Aers takes as his starting point the social, political and cultural context of any writing, indicating the need to attempt an understanding of that context, to try to recreate its historical background, before any exploration of the texts it has produced might begin. His argument here is that authors bring to their writings a set of ideas, opinions, values or prejudices that have been determined by the culture of their time. He believes that writing does not appear in a vacuum but is shaped by the experiences of its authors. He is thus adopting an historical or historicist approach which inevitably suggests that his prime concern is with social and political systems. This very concern, plus the language in which he couches that concern, might nevertheless indicate to you that his own bias is a political one.

Aers also writes,

> For all reconstruction is undertaken with a subjectivity shaped by the specific social world in and through which we have been able to develop our very consciousness and identity, let alone our habits of reading. The reader is a product of the cultural system within which she or he reads, however heterogeneous and differentiated this system may be. (Aers, 1986: 5)

Here the stress upon 'reader' indicates a belief that the relationship between a text and its audience is vital, for the reader, or listener, is also a product of a system and has their own in-built experiences and beliefs to contend with. What effects do you think such a belief might have upon your own reading of Chaucer? How is it possible for you as a product of the twentieth century – with its insistence upon equality between the sexes, an ambiguous relationship with God, a belief in the individual and his/her rights, and an entirely different social and political system – to read this medieval author with any understanding of the issues raised in his work? Equally, can you perceive in Chaucer's writing a response to the demands of *his* audience, or a response to the social and cultural concerns of his day?

With this in mind, Aers argues for the need to read openly, to be prepared to suspend our own values and expectations so that our reading is

> ...informed by a serious attempt to reconstruct the text's moment of production, its own contexts of discourse and social practices within and for which it achieved meaning. (Aers, 1986: 6)

At the same time he suggests a need to read 'reflexively', and to ground our reading in both the historical and individual consciousness of the author and his time, as well as remaining aware of *our* time and culture and of our own selves. The danger lies in attempting to do what is traditional, which is to objectify texts and their traditions, or to see them as authoritative with their ideas and values 'reified', to use this critic's terminology. To read reflexively or openly is to destroy that notion of authority according to Aers. Thus,

> Reflexive imagination returns reified texts and authorities to their human speakers, disclosed with their inevitable limitations and partial interests. (Aers, 1980: 83)

To what extent is such a view applicable to Chaucer in your opinion? Was he also attempting to fracture authoritative notions of what literature should be or what it should be about? Another point worth bearing in mind is the extent to which Aers himself may be guilty of failing to read in the very way he advocates. He has a vested left-wing bias which you probably spotted earlier. Is it enough that it is a declared and openly acknowledged interest, or does it mean that in some ways he is always seeking a criticism of, or even rebellion against, a dominant or accepted ideology? It is a question to which you may wish to return at the end of this section.

Aers advocates that Chaucer was well placed to practise this reflexive approach because he was determined to engage with certain aspects of his culture including its ideology and social practices. He believes that his writings examine, rather than simply repeat, authoritative and dominant traditions. In particular, he thinks that Chaucer's imagination as a writer was concerned with fundamental questions of knowledge and authority, and that he wished to show the processes by which that authority was constructed as well as the ways it remained rooted in both individual and social worlds (Aers, 1980: 81–2]. Thus Chaucer's writing was marked by an openness to and awareness of the shifting and contradictory forces of his time (Aers, 1986: 15). How far does this correspond to your own reading of Chaucer? Look at the prologues of the Wife of Bath and the

Pardoner, for example, and then compare them to the *Merchant's Tale* or the *Shipman's Tale*.

An important question remains and that is how Aers applies his theories to his chosen texts. In one example, the *Nun's Priest's*, he uses the tale to demonstrate the way appeals to authority only work when 'there is a consensus in the community' (Aers, 1986: 10) about which texts count as authority, and how they should be read or interpreted. In the light of this, reconsider the argument between Chauntecleer and Pertelote concerning the interpretation of the former's dream, as well as the opening to the *Wife of Bath's Prologue*, where she contemplates a range of traditional authorities explained by clerics and, contrasting them with her own experience, gives them her own unique interpretation.

Let us begin, however, with a consideration of the following statement:

> Chaucer's poetry dramatises the way a market society dissolves such traditional ideology and its ethical discourses while it shapes human relationships around the exchange of commodities. His work evokes human agents for whom traditional ideas of community and common profit are irrelevant anachronisms. (Aers, 1986: 20)

The language of this statement is straight out of a sociological textbook and, as such, resistant to interpretation. What do you think Aers means? Again it is a question to keep in mind during the following explorations of two figures who appear crucial to any demonstration of this critic's ideas, who, in spite of or even because of the fact that they are regarded as problematical voices within the *Tales* as a whole, seem to dominate discussion.

According to Aers, the figure of the Pardoner allows Chaucer to undermine any 'uncritical acceptance of authority' for the images, language and practices described separate the spiritual or the ideal from 'the social, economic and material dimensions of human being' (Aers, 1986: 51). It is Chaucer's creation of this 'difficult' voice that offers an example of the ways in which 'Chaucer's works contain many examples of the de-sublimation of reified discourse, retrieving the specific human speakers who have become occluded.' (Aers,

1980: 88) What Aers seems to be suggesting is that the existence of this complex figure enables Chaucer to criticise some of the religious practices with which the Pardoner is involved, as well as demonstrating the corrosive effects of the Pardoner's occupation upon his own personality. Thus he is not merely an odd or perverted individual but an example of someone who has recognised that gap between ideal and practice mentioned in previous chapters, a gap that Chaucer himself is anxious to explore.

Detailed discussion of the *Pardoner's Prologue* focuses upon his revelation and enjoyment of his own role, as well as his awareness of his audience's relish for his preaching display. Aers refers closely to the text to support his views. In particular he mentions the Pardoner's outline of what he does in order to encourage the people to offer money to him (VI (C) ll.329–65 and ll.389–438). In this way Chaucer 'shows us the presence of creating *self* and the centrality of aesthetic dimensions in the discourse of the church's preachers'. By offering this exaggerated and amusing revelation and foregrounding the activity of the individual in this process, Aers claims that Chaucer is able to provoke detachment from the teaching and authority of those preachers, instead of the uncritical acceptance the tradition demanded and usually received (Aers, 1980: 92). Aers argues that an audience that responds thoughtfully to the Pardoner's self-awareness as he tells how he creates his own role, might have begun to question the very phrases and symbols traditionally used in such discourse. Aers cites the moment when the Pardoner describes his own nodding head, neck outstretched like a barn-dove to survey his audience, as an example of this, suggesting that attention is drawn to the traditional symbol of the biblical dove. In this way what ought to be spiritual becomes material, or matter, thus opening up a challenge and a parallel; the Pardoner's spiritual function is denied and replaced with a worldly or temporal one.

Similarly, the Pardoner tells how he uses Latin to stir the audience to devotion. This traditional 'high' Church language established its (clerical) speakers as separate to the inferior lay folk listening to the sermon. Aers suggests that the next time this is heard, rather than 'confirming the preacher's impersonality and superior knowledge, it encourages the listener to speculate about the motivation of the individual exalted in the pulpit', for now the audience might be more aware that this sort of language is used in a dramatic performance designed to get their money rather than save their souls (Aers, 1980: 93).

Aers also believes that it is impossible to dismiss the Pardoner or dilute his threat to the established order by seeing him as deviant or simply an odd individual. Chaucer's attack is not upon the man but upon the *practice* of pardoners, upon the way they acted as official agents of the Church. His criticism is of the authority or institution employing him to do a job from which that institution stands to gain monetary reward. Thus when the Pardoner tells his pilgrim audience exactly how he does it, even trying to extract money from them at the end, he is acknowledging 'his own complicity in the dominant institution, the attitudes and values it shares with the secular world' (Aers, 1980: 95). What Chaucer is doing in this text is using the Pardoner's 'self-reflexivity to unmask the dominant practices and values of the orthodox institution which claimed a monopoly on the means of grace and correct doctrine' (Aers, 1980: 96).

At the end of his *Prologue* the Pardoner calls the pilgrims to come and offer to his relics or ask him to pardon their sins. Frequently critics argue that the character is simply carried away by his own eloquence at this point. For Aers, though, it is a deliberate move indicating a complete awareness of what he is doing. The offer is mocking for it reminds everyone what he is and the means by which the institution they trust in works. Here he deliberately steps out of the role of storyteller and into his role as a pardoner, a neat irony considering the context of pilgrimage in the dramatic frame of the *Tales*. (Aers, 1980: 98–9). In these closing lines Aers believes that Chaucer targets several areas through the voice of the Pardoner. One is the Church itself which gives the Pardoner the authority to sell his pardons. Another is the self-seeking and gullible audience who mingle superstition and materialism with their Christian faith, both revering and fearing the Church's authority. Yet another is the Pardoner himself because he depends on both the Church and his audience for his employment, but despises them both.

His revelation succeeds, however, in drawing attention to the way the Church constantly stimulated guilt and a religious anxiety in its followers which could only be assuaged by constantly paying the very institution 'designed' to save those unworthy souls (Aers, 1980: 100). It remains a comic portrait, the humour arising from the Pardoner's awareness of how the system works and his own role in it. His vision may have been a distorted one, says Aers, but the Pardoner retained a sharp awareness of his own culture, one which Chaucer highlights. For this critic then this tale shows how 'religion could be made into a commodity' where even its language is financial, and where spiritual values like 'goode' and 'trewe' are used by the Pardoner as measures of money (Aers, 1980: 101).

If at this point we reconsider the earlier quotation in which Aers speaks of market forces and the way that traditional ideas (even language) shape human relationships, it might now be possible to see more clearly what he means by this. His interpretation of the Pardoner centres upon his two roles, as an agent of the Church collecting money, and a character whose own 'reflexivity', or openness to ideas, sets him apart from others. The Pardoner realises exactly what he is up to when he performs his duties; further, he knows precisely the means by which he is so successful. He knows, if Aers is to be believed, what the Church requires of him, (i.e. to make money), what his audience likes, and how clever he is at satisfying the demands of both. It is a mutual activity shaped around an exchange of 'commodities', where everyone gets what they want, including his audiences who believe themselves absolved of sin. It is also an activity focused upon the driving force, not of God or grace, but of money. Chaucer thus uses the figure of the Pardoner to dramatise and criticise this neglect of spiritual values. An extremely self-aware and reflexive character, the Pardoner is nevertheless a voice or an agent for Chaucer's ideas, as well as an example of how his writing opens up alternative perspectives. Aers offers an interpretation that highlights the social world of Chaucer's time, an activity that he repeats with the Wife of Bath.

Aers suggests that the *Wife of Bath's Prologue* is also an invitation by Chaucer to subvert the existing order. Her comments on texts and stories are a challenge to authority and established doctrines of all kinds, but especially ecclesiastical. He argues that she returns these authorities to history, demonstrating that they are only the product of human individuals or groups, and so marked by their own interests or prejudices (Aers, 1980: 83). In her *Prologue* she is highly critical of these interests and authorities, but the paradox for Aers is that she also accepts these traditions; her first four marriages, for example, are contracted for money not love. Thus she accepts that the basis of marriage is an economic one. Aers similarly indicates that the Wife rejects the role of the passive woman in no uncertain terms with her insistence on and depiction of her attempts to gain 'maistrie', yet, at the same time, her 'becoming' the dominant partner (in effect the husband) affirms the existing culture (Aers, 1980: 148).

His proof of this view is supported by the text itself. He begins by discussing the moment when Alison declares God's purpose in making the sexual organs of men and women (III (D) ll.115–30). Aers argues that

> she begins by failing to distinguish the different potentials of sexual organs and labels them members 'of generacion'. (l. 116) This classification undermines her case before her argument is even launched, revealing the power of 'auctoritee' in moulding her perceptions and reasoning about her 'experience', for there she has lived through very definite distinctions between dutiful wifely copulation and the kind of joyful love-making she describes in her fifth marriage (Aers, 1986: 148).

Here he suggests that although Alison's own experience of sexual joy in a loving relationship tells her otherwise, and although her intention is to criticise the accepted or orthodox view – that sexual pleasure is neither possible nor desirable – her very terminology betrays the extent to which she has swallowed these teachings. He continues by pointing out that she mocks those who describe sexual organs as gender determinate or intended to fulfil biological necessities such as the relieving of the bladder, again making her appeal to the 'experience' of sex. Yet, says Aers, Chaucer demonstrates how she has been taken over by the received wisdom or authority of her time when she claims that, in order to avoid clerical displeasure, she will concede that they are made for both, for 'office and fore ese/Of engendrure' (ll.127–8).

He draws attention to the syntax of this passage as an example of how Chaucer uses it to show the Wife's train of thought. Aers writes,

> The first two lines take up her appeal to 'experience' against 'the clerkes' and promise to state her own meaning explicitly. The next line seems to fulfil this promise: 'they maked ben...for ese'. Here, we feel, the rebellious Wife makes her stand. Despite the opening classification, she now places sheer *ese* as one of God's aims in giving humans their sexuality. The 'clerkes' are put in their place. But not for long, since the next lines force us to re-interpret and qualify 'ese' in a strictly orthodox sense – 'ese/Of engendrure'. The Wife's 'experience' of sexual pleasure as an end in itself within her fifth marriage collapses into the traditional clerkly orthodoxy regarding sexual intercourse. After this it is no surprise to see her move on to the second orthodox purpose of marriage, according to what 'men...in hir bookes sette': to make 'paiement' of the marital 'dette' (ll.129–32). Nor is it a surprise that she concludes with further confirmation of the ideological orthodoxies against which she is overtly in rebellion: 'Thanne were they maad...To purge uryne, and eek for engendrure (ll.113–14). (Aers, 1986: 149)

What the Wife says at this point, as well as how she expresses it, demonstrates for Aers the near-impossibility of escaping received ideas and orthodoxies by using a different, 'new' language. All that happens is that the values are so imbued in Alison, and in people generally, that it is tradition which is finally affirmed; love, sex, and marriage fail to be integrated. The evidence that Aers offers for his assertion that the Wife is ultimately unable to escape orthodox thought, and that she continues to mirror its ideas, might be described as overwhelming. Just as traditional authority has it that love and sex are mutually exclusive, Alison separates them too. She speaks of her 'queynte' always on offer to her men, and tells how she could never withdraw her 'chambre of Venus from a good felawe' (ll.149–57, 331–5, and 618). Aers notes that here her sexuality is presented in the abstract and the impersonal, adding

> This fragmentation and depersonalisation of sex separates it from any constant and total human love, and is actually the very image of orthodox ecclesiastical tradition. (Aers, 1986: 150)

Aers accepts that Alison also retains a self-awareness seen in her craving for love, and the way she movingly recalls her past life as well as recounting her present. Her final marriage is an attempt to reconcile what medieval orthodox teaching separated – love, sex, and marriage. Widowed several times over and a wealthy woman in her own right, she is finally able to choose freely her next spouse whom she takes 'for love', not money. Yet Aers believes that she continues to see all in terms of economics, as an exchange of commodities, even though this is exactly what she is rebelling against. Alison perpetuates the outlook and practices which she seeks to deny, for

> Chaucer's imagination was so engaged with the realities of his own culture in relation to the Wife's consciousness and actions that he did not allow the fifth marriage to achieve any straightforward transcendence of these realities. (Aers, 1986: 150)

In my opinion Aers neatly avoids the danger of discussing this persuasive figure as a fully realised human being with a life of her own beyond the text; she is not in any way 'alive', though she is extremely lifelike, but exists as a product of Chaucer's manipulation of his art, a 'voice', a vehicle for his poetic skill and ideas, just as the Pardoner is. He suggests that Chaucer, once again, engages with the pervasive power of the very culture the Wife attempts to oppose, thus demonstrating the way it has shaped and dominated individuals' values and expectations. At the same time, Chaucer is able to criticise those values.

In further 'proof' of his argument, Aers cites the way Alison surrenders 'al the lond and fee' to this last husband exactly in accordance with the usual tradition. Her husband's reaction to her love and generosity is domineering, just as convention demands. His anti-feminist appeals to authority are then satirized by Chaucer, while the very manner of the husband's speech permits no reply, and allows no other perspective; it is this that Chaucer's own poetry opposes. Alison's fight to retain control similarly illustrates the masculine-dominated norms that she mistakenly thinks her actions have broken. Once again Aers draws attention to language in his careful and persuasive close reading, indicating that the Wife uses the traditional imagery of one partner, usually the male, as a rider and the other, the woman, as an animal requiring control. She achieves power by gaining the 'bridel' but merely inverts traditions of dominance. Aers implies that she is finally unable to change or replace these traditions, believing himself not guilty of the usual critical responses to the Wife at this point which attack her as a woman, a character. Instead he says,

> Chaucer has enacted a highly critical and dramatic reflection on orthodox marital ideologies and practices showing us how difficult it is to transcend them even when they are experienced as gravely inadequate. (Aers, 1986: 151)

Summary

The approach taken by David Aers is one which insists that Chaucer's work is placed in its historical context and read reflexively or with an open mind, aware of personal prejudices or vested interests. His focus is upon Chaucer as a critical commentator of his time. Thus his critical perspective is a political one emphasising social, cultural and economic interests, focused on the power of dominant institutions, and the way ordinary people respond to this. He is a highly complex critic, able to offer some brilliant insights into individual tales as well as into our own approaches to reading and understanding texts.

Some questions remain to be asked, however. How far does his approach illuminate all texts? Consider the extent to which the *Miller's Tale* or the *Reeve's* is able to support a sociological reading. What, if anything, is Chaucer criticising in these tales? If you extend your reading to the *Clerk's Tale*, do you agree that its focus is upon notions of lordship and feudal power? Does an insistence upon this socio-political approach close down your reading by ignoring other concerns? For example, Aers quite rightly identifies the problems of 'voice' raised in the Pardoner and the Wife, but does he acknowledge the multiplicity of voices seen right across the *Tales* or in Chaucer's other writings, let alone in his development of the role of the narrator? How can his critical perspective 'answer' the tale of *Sir Thopas*? Does his insistence upon dividing the *Tales* into thematic areas or topics fully recognise the intertextuality of the whole web of stories?

Finally, consider the extent to which Aers satisfies his own notion of reflexivity as well as the possibility that his approach requires a great deal of prior historical knowledge to make sense of these works.

ELAINE TUTTLE HANSEN[8]

It is the very title of Hansen's book, *Chaucer and the Fictions of Gender*, that initially reveals her interest in Chaucer. Its focus is upon the word 'fictions', indicating both an awareness of the act of writing and the sense that things are not quite as secure or obvious as they seem. Her second word, 'gender', reveals her approach and concerns. It is a judgement supported by a quick glance at the terminology she tends to employ, language once again offering clues to critical perspective. Contemplate the use of words such as 'heterosexual', 'feminisation', 'manliness', 'power', 'gender', 'gender roles', 'gender difference', 'maleness', 'masculine', 'feminine', 'marginalised', 'suppression', or 'orthodox authorities'. What do they suggest to you? If you assumed that her stance is a feminist one you would be correct, but closer examination of her terminology, as well as the title of her book, should also indicate a qualification of this original starting point.

Hansen's concern is with Chaucer's 'feminisation' of *men*. She begins her argument with an exploration of what she perceives as a crucial work, namely *The Legend of Good Women*. It is this poem that she regards as holding the thread of Chaucer's interest in the presentation of men *and* women, and the way that they conduct their relationships. She suggests that, despite its title, this poem is not a work about women but about men, for heterosexual love involves men in a loss of manliness as the stories' heroes are portrayed as victims, like women, of a love that turns *them* into liars, storytellers (an activity associated with the feminine), or betrayers. In these legends, apparently told in defence of women, fathers act upon their sons just as they do upon their daughters, failing to protect them or else invoking some upset or confrontation that works to the sons' detriment. Hansen concludes that when Chaucer focuses upon women it is not because he is pro-female but because he wishes to open up the problem of 'false' men, masculine imagination, and male authorship. She believes that though Chaucer represents women and appears to speak in their defence against the prevailing orthodoxy of his time, no female voices are, in fact, heard, as it is not their concerns that stimulate his interest but something more general. Chaucer's representations of women remain slippery for Hansen who argues that Chaucer uses them and the cultural problems of his time to open up other problems and perspectives, not least concerns about his own writing as a male author (Hansen, 1992: 12). What do you make of the following lengthy extract from Hansen?

> I have stressed, then, that in the very real continuity of concern throughout Chaucerian fiction with the representation of women, I hear not a swelling chorus of female voices entering the text and speaking for and about themselves, but something of a monotone making known both feminine absence and masculine anxiety. As I listen, what often sounds like a woman's voice, what is spoken in the name of women inflected by different and highly realistic, sometimes subversive, dialects, always enters and leaves Chaucerian story not as the enunciation of an autonomous speaker, but as an urgent problem for the gendered identity of male characters, male narrators, and (?male) readers. The problem is always represented in large part as a problem of the feminization of men. The repetitive return to the fraught depiction of women and of male speakers, characters, and narrators alike, who in various ways resemble those women, in turn documents the dubious nature of gender difference. (Hansen,1992: 12)

There are several points to consider in this statement. Perhaps the first thing to note is Hansen's use of 'hear' and 'listen', indicating an approach that looks beneath the surface narrative, and is searching for something implicit or hidden behind the dominant text. The second is that, like Aers, she recognises the existence of some very realistic or human-sounding voices, the Wife of Bath maybe, that do not, however, have an independent life of their own but remain a fiction, part of Chaucer's imagination. Those same voices, whether male or female, are also only *apparently* centred upon the plight of women in an anti-feminist society. In reality, they are inextricably linked to the masculine, in the way that men are represented *as* men, or the way that male narrators or writers might present themselves. Hansen sees a similarity in Chaucer's writing between the presentation of men and women; they are alike and this similarity highlights the slipperiness of fixed notions of gender, suggesting that gender roles are not always as secure or definite as they might seem.

It is important to identify exactly what Hansen means by 'feminisation'. She indicates that she does not intend this to be understood as the emasculation of men, but as a sort of role reversal whereby men become similar to either women or what is traditionally regarded as feminine. She writes,

> To speak of feminisation is on the contrary to suggest that the feminine, in this cultural context a pejorative mark and a set of subordinated or marginalised positions historically occupied most often by female human beings, may have a certain potency and priority, although this possibility is just what it is repeatedly necessary to disprove. (Hansen, 1992: 17)

A focus upon women and the problems experienced by them in the profoundly misogynist culture of medieval times does not, says Hansen, resolve those problems. Instead, it demonstrates how men and women might be compared to each other, and how men are Chaucer's real concern (Hansen, 1992: 17). He is able to focus upon this by using in his work the pervasive and negative influence of the cultural presentation of women or their function.

Is Hansen a feminist? Despite what her ideas might suggest, she is, but her approach is one of caution. She reminds us of the historical context of the time, and in some ways possibly might be commended for her reflexive (to use David Aers's terminology) or realistic perspective. What she does not do is impose her own contemporary Western ideals upon Chaucer's work, however tempting this might be. She agrees that it is a relatively rare occasion when Chaucer centres upon women or presents us with a female speaker;

at least this demonstrates that, unlike most of his contemporaries, he is prepared to open up and perhaps question the prevalent misogyny of his time (Hansen, 1992: 286). With this in mind, examine some of the tales in which he might be said to do this. The *Wife of Bath's Tale* and *Prologue* are obvious examples but what about the presentation of Emily in the *Knight's Tale*, Alison in the *Miller's* or May in the *Merchant's*, let alone Custance in the *Man of Law's Tale* and Griselda in the *Clerk's*?

Hansen believes, though, that Chaucer remains part of the *status quo*, 'a personality who seeks to enjoy all the material and symbolic privileges of maleness, while transcending the constraints of "the body writing" to grasp the otherwise unavailable, to take a neutral or universally human position' (Hansen, 1992: 286–7). In order to understand Chaucer's work we should consider its context, and thus she draws attention to medieval notions of gender[9] as well as that world's acceptance of and engagement with gender problems. The medieval period was not 'a monolithic block of placid submission to orthodox authorities', and if we are unable to hear women's voices, at least we can identify 'men's concern' (Hansen, 1992: 287). Such a view might imply that feminist approaches to authors like Chaucer are simply not viable, let alone worthwhile, but Hansen again qualifies her comments. Though advocating caution, she suggests that Chaucer can 'still be read and valued for his humanist insight and sympathy for the female as well as his dispassionate artistic greatness' (Hansen, 1992: 44). What is implied in this remark, however, is a separation between Chaucer the writer or artist and Chaucer the man; is Hansen trying to have it both ways, and does the text support a split between the two? Is it at all possible (or desirable) to identify Chaucer the man? She continues, noting that even though Chaucer's representations of men and women 'are deployed as the battleground over which authority, selfhood, and unity can be established', he at least begins to question things, to look at the world from the standpoint of those excluded from it, silenced, and for whom his texts were not actually written (Hansen, 1992: 292). Do you agree with this?

Hansen argues that Chaucer's central concern is not social criticism as Aers believes, but writing itself. Chaucer's focus is frequently upon the narrators or speakers of his tales, while any depiction of women is really a portrayal of what it might mean to be a man. She argues that Chaucer demonstrates that ideals concerning adult male power are unattainable for most men, while 'such power is itself, like clear gender distinctions, unstable, even illusory, at the same time that both the constraints and uncertainties of gender roles are inescapable'. What men fear most in Chaucer's works is that they might actually be women (Hansen, 1992: 288). Once again it might be useful to bear in mind this last remark as we begin an examination of how Hansen applies her ideas to the texts themselves.

Unlike many traditional critics Hansen does not read the Wife of Bath as a domineering figure, but as 'a dramatic and important instance of woman's silence and suppression in history and language' (Hansen, 1992: 27–8). She suggests that in the *Prologue* what is revealed is the power of language as a weapon that might afford the Wife of Bath some control, just as Alison uses sex and money to achieve a measure of independent power (Hansen, 1992: 28). Like Aers, Hansen believes that the *Prologue's* citation of authorities shows how she is *acted upon* as she is forced to defend herself against a vague and unnameable, but huge, force of social disapproval; what Alison is unable to do is pin it down and fight it. Hence she understands its hostility but not the meaning of the arguments against her. She struggles to give it meaning – her own – but is unable to clarify or oppose it (Hansen, 1992: 30).

A brief examination of what Alison actually says might be used to support Hansen's assertion here. The Wife pits her own 'experience' against what men tell her when they 'glose' authoritative texts. She challenges,

'Wher can ye seye, in any manere age
That hye God defended mariage
By expres word? I pray yow, telleth me.
Or where comanded he virginitee?'

(III (D) ll.59–61)

From there she goes on to question a whole range of masculine teachings (ll.1–162), yet continues to use, according to Hansen, the same language and the same range of ideas used by those authorities themselves. In particular, Hansen draws attention to the point at which Alison rages against the fact that it is men who write stories, and men who defame women; if women had been given such an opportunity they might have spoken in their turn of the wickedness of men. Alison cries, 'Who peyntede the leon, tel me who?' (ll.692–96) This involuntary cry of anger, as Hansen terms it, comes from the same patriarchal culture against which she rails, meeting like with like; if men wish to close down the possibility of all argument by authoritatively declaring against women, then, advocates Alison, we women shall do the same. It is only a vague and hostile response to the vague and hostile threat she feels she faces, and, as such, solves nothing. Hansen argues that when the question is asked 'who painted the lion?' the Wife is asking 'from whose viewpoint is this story being told?'

Hansen believes this is a central question. The Wife indicates that if women were allowed to tell stories then they would be different to men's – or, in fact, exactly the same, expressing anxieties about gender differences and the battle between the sexes. Yet, at the same time, her comment reminds us that at the centre of this drama is that selfsame question, for it is Chaucer, not the human and lifelike figure of the Wife, who tells this story. Thus a male author has created this 'woman' and given her these lines to speak. Like every other female character or speaker, says Hansen, Alison exists only in Chaucer's imagination, and so this 'monster' can never, as is so frequently assumed, speak on behalf of women. Chaucer is filtering voices and ideas, as Alison's own question reminds us, but as a woman she would not be allowed a voice at all; her very gender excludes the possibility of her telling any stories in this public arena. She, like all women, is in fact absent from her own story and her own life. Even as she speaks, she remains outside the bounds of both language and literary convention (Hansen, 1992: 34–5).

Though I have simplified Hansen's terminology, if not her ideas, this remains an interesting response to the difficulties compounded by Chaucer's use of this speaker, one identified as problematical in earlier chapters. To what extent do you agree with it? Does it illuminate in any way what Hansen has to say about the instability of gender difference, or does it simply highlight her notion that men, and above all writing, remain the central concerns of much of Chaucer's work? Hansen, like Aers, seems to be suggesting that the Wife is so imbued with the values of the society she attempts to criticise that she is unable to stand back from it, and merely reinforces, or reifies, the very power that she intends to undermine. Such a belief almost precludes the possibility of any feminist interpretation of such a text for it implies that any struggle is futile. Do you agree with this? What about the possibility that the use of the very language and ideas of the dominant (masculine) culture demonstrates the extent to which the female has learned its rules so well that she is able to criticise it from within; it is not that she is unable to free herself from it but that such a subversion is more likely to succeed than open rebellion. Interestingly Hansen does not consider such an idea.

Equally contentious is Hansen's view of the *Miller's Tale.* Her starting point is that this poem is far from the innocent celebration of life so many critics speak of, but contains, in fact, a dark aspect to its comedy. One of the ways in which this is seen is through an exploration of the moments towards the end of the tale, and the issue of what is commonly referred to as the 'misdirected kiss'. (I (A) ll.3714–3813)

Hansen opens her discussion by reference to the ambiguity of the term 'hole' – that which Alison exposes to Absolon at the window. She asks if this means 'anus' or 'vagina', suggesting that most assume the former, thus associating a woman's sex, or sex with a woman, with 'dirt, decay, and dissolution' (Hansen, 1992: 277). She suggests that the audience receives 'a shocking encounter with female dirt and danger that both sickens and (therefore) heals the lovesick man' (Hansen, 1992: 228). The tale relates how Absolon's love turns cold at this point, and he is cured of it. Hansen argues that the tone and intention of the tale shift at this moment. She notes that earlier there was no hesitation in identifying Alison's 'queynte'; here, the reference is an obscene one referring to her vagina. Later, that same female part is described as a 'hole' or anus, that part which both men and women share, and *not* the 'queynte', mark of female difference. At the same time Nicholas's body is substituted for Alison's at the window, 'a maneuver that returns agency to the male but in doing so also exposes the humiliating and frightening lack of difference between male and female bodies' (Hansen, 1992: 228).

You can probably already anticipate the line of Hansen's argument here as she firmly relates this tale to her proposal that Chaucer's concern is not with women but with men, with the instability of gender boundaries, and with the feminisation of men. Much of the tale's humour at this moment is derived from the earlier strong indications that there is more than a hint of the effeminate in Absolon. His lack of experience with women leads to his confusion and great shock when he finally kisses Alison. He thinks that he is aware of a beard, a sign of the male. Hansen wonders whether he fears he has kissed a man, a fear later 'confirmed' by the substitution of Nicholas for Alison. His confusion is compounded as he hears Alison laughing and Nicholas 'repeating' his fear with the words 'A berd, a berd!' (ll.3742) Here 'beard' becomes practical joke.

Absolon's response is explored by Hansen who suggests that his hysterical rubbing of his lips once he realises what has actually happened to him adds to the notion of Alison as dirt. He vows revenge and weeps like a child (ll.3759), a simile that Hansen finds telling, a hint that Absolon is 'infantilized and punished' by this contact, is 'like the putatively generic little boy who sees female genitals for the first time' and responds in a manner indicating 'both guilt and fear for his own as yet unproven difference and dominance, his phallus' (Hansen, 1992: 230).

Hansen's use of Freudian terminology is off-putting, but what she seems to be suggesting is that Absolon is unsure of his own adult sexuality. It is not simply that he fears he may be homosexual, though this is present as a possibility, according to Hansen. It is also that he has not yet proved himself as worthy of the 'phallus', or has not yet proved his manliness. Combined with his earlier confusion and the switch between Nicholas and Alison, his reaction is part of what is most disturbing, and that is the fear that men and women may not actually be so very different. Hansen relates two things to exemplify this fear. The first is Absolon's fear of castration or homosexuality. The second is the possible rape or mutilation of Alison. The two are brought out in an exploration of Absolon's revenge.

Absolon borrows a red-hot 'kultour' (iron blade at the front end of a plough) from the very masculine blacksmith;

> he borrows the violent maleness, the-phallus-as-weapon, that the coulter symbolizes simultaneously to avenge and display his vulnerable manhood...Absolon realigns himself with the phallic miller, who ambiguously swears that he won't believe he's a cuckold 'for the oxen in my plogh' (l.3159). (Hansen, 1992: 231)

However, he is fooled again. Hansen clarifies her position at this point. She declares that his reaction to the first time Alison presents her 'hole' rather than her mouth indicates that his effeminacy is an external sign of 'the precariousness of masculine desire'. The second time, when it is Nicholas's 'hole' that is presented, means that Absolon is unable to affirm his masculinity by violently assaulting the woman responsible for his humiliation. Hansen writes,

> It is no accident that the actual recipient of Absolon's blade – the surrogate of his imagined, frustrated desire for a woman – is a man, and a man in a social position very similar to his own in many ways; and this turn of events has several interesting consequences. It frustrates the effort to prove manliness and emphasizes the ambiguities of gender difference, and it further unmans and humiliates the effeminate male both by demonstrating that he is not even capable of taking revenge against a woman and by forcing him to engage unwittingly in an act that must suggest sodomy. (Hansen, 1992: 232)

She indicates that this cruel and vicious act is usually overlooked in the tale. Yet it remains an example of misogyny that at the same time affirms the centrality and power of women. It is an issue not really taken up in the story for Nicholas intervenes in the plot and so reasserts the male as the real social and moral agent. Hansen also notes that Nicholas is not, as most assume, the exact opposite of his rival and therefore unequivocally manly, for, at the same time as he 'quites' Absolon by pretending to be Alison, he acts out a 'feminisation', a fear of the homo-erotic. Nicholas's own masculinity is also called into question.

To begin with, his private parts are substituted for Alison's; in the dark, says Hansen, the two become interchangeable and gender difference is blurred. He too is feminised. He is 'sleigh and ful privee' (l.3201), a secrecy associated with the woman's 'pryvetee' (or sex) in the Miller's opening lines. He is also typically clerkly, like a meek maiden (l.3202). His lust for Alison seems to contradict this but it might be argued that he is more interested in his own cleverness, his own ability to 'quite' John the carpenter. Hansen argues that the repetitive rhyme conflates female genitals and 'clerkly ingenuity':

> ...'this hende Nicholas
> Fil with this yonge wyf to rage and pleye,
> Whil that hir housbonde was at Oseneye,
> As clerkes ben ful subtile and ful queynte;
> And prively he caughte hir by the queynte.' (ll.3173–6)

Nicholas is given a chance to prove that he is 'queynte' (clever or sly) by outwitting John and thus the 'energy of the narration in the tale matches and defines the energy of Nicholas not as sexual but as authorial'. Nicholas spends ages planning the elaborate hoax, all for one night with his beloved, a sexual encounter described in less than ten lines (ll.3650–6) (Hansen, 1992: 234).

For Hansen, then, what this tale is about is Chaucer's fiction-making. Though Nicholas is feminised in some respects, he also reinforces gender 'hierarchy' and ensures that, once again, it is men who are important. Thus he substitutes himself for Alison's 'hole', makes the use of this word less ambiguous for it is *his* 'hole' that is important, just as it is men who are the important agents in the story. Alison is shoved to the margins of the action, and made into a passive character as befits the traditional depiction of women; we are told that 'Thus swyved is this carpenteris wyf' (l.3850) who escapes all retribution in the closing moments of the tale. Hansen draws attention to this line, once again offering a very close reading of it. She suggests,

> Nature's female has suddenly become the grammatical object of the verb and a nameless possession of her husband in a way that does not seem to reflect what we saw earlier of Alisoun any more than it supports a reading of her as 'triumphant'.

At the same time the tale remains an example of the threat to masculinity where Absolon's violent and fearful response to the woman is obscured, and Nicholas's branding so nearly causes his castration (Hansen, 1992: 235).

Summary

Hansen's approach to Chaucer's work relies very heavily upon a close and careful reading, only some of which has been outlined here. Her interests are gender and gender identity, and, as such, she focuses upon the presentation of both men and women, concluding, in spite of her own feminist tendencies, that Chaucer's real concern is with the latter. Some of her material is very complicated, but her readings are consistently 'new' and stimulating.

As you formulate your own opinion of her critical perspective, consider some of the following questions. Does her heavy qualification of a feminist approach, and her suggestion that many issues merely serve to bolster the masculine-dominated system apparently under attack, invalidate a female-centred perspective? Does her concern with gender narrow her readings of these tales? Is Hansen guilty of partial readings or ignoring the intertextuality of the whole set of *Tales*? Do her views illuminate other stories? What about the *Merchant's Tale* or the *Reeve's* and *Shipman's*? Is it at all possible to read the *Nun's Priest's Tale* in this light, particularly the relationship between Chauntecleer and Pertelote? How, if at all, is it helpful in reading the *Pardoner's Tale* or his *Prologue?*

HELEN COOPER[10]

Very different from the previous pair of critics, Cooper's approach is revealed in a terminology that centres upon words like 'stories', 'associations', 'genre', 'traditions', 'dramatically', 'thematically', 'fragments', 'voices', 'narrative layers', 'intertextuality', and 'juxtaposition'. Her concern is with the *Tales* as a whole, with the ways in which stories interweave and multiply, with Chaucer's notion of order and purpose in writing them, and with, as her title, *The Structure of 'The Canterbury Tales'*, suggests, the structure and purpose of this set of disparate stories. As such she is far less concerned with close textual analysis of individual tales and much more aware of an overview.

The thrust of Cooper's argument is that Chaucer was essentially writing in the genre of story-collection, where individual tales are connected by some greater or wider notion, and, though they may be read individually, actually belong together. She advocates the need to examine these interrelationships between different stories as well as between different types of stories and different narratorial voices. In addition, she draws our attention to the importance of the dramatic frame, and to the problems aroused by its partial or incomplete realisation. She also insists upon an exploration of the order or fragments these tales were arranged in, together with the links between themes, common topics, or ideas. The hallmark of her approach is cross-referencing and interweaving. Cooper claims that the *Tales*

> is a particularly fascinating example of how conventions work, for Chaucer is able to set up multiple layers of reference. Every genre he uses – and he uses just about every one available to him – brings its own associations and traditions; and in addition, by bringing together so many stories of so many different kinds, he is able to play off associations between the tales within the work. (Cooper, 1983: 4–5)

Cooper begins by examining the story-collection as a genre in an attempt to define the parameters of her own work, as well as to say how it might have functioned generally. She looks at its popularity and the influences on Chaucer of previous story-collection authors such as Boccaccio and Gower. Whilst it remains a miscellany, it is also a genre in its own right with individual authors imposing their own different kind of order upon it. In essence it is a collection of individual tales compiled and written or rewritten by a single author, and circulated as one document or text (Cooper, 1983: 9). Medieval audiences would have been entirely familiar with such a genre; what is perhaps difficult for us is that we are not, and hence see in the incomplete, fragmentary nature of the work, its conflicting voices, and inconsistent use of a dramatic frame an artistic failure, a potential weakness, or something problematical in a manner over and above what might be expected.

Cooper does not seek to minimise these difficulties, but restates or repositions them. She agrees that as a single collection or poem the work is incomplete, and that though its frame is a storytelling contest its rules are applied inconsistently for there is no outcome or winner, and not every character tells a tale; in fact, some never 'speak' at all while others, who do not appear in the *General Prologue*, participate in the game. At the same time the *Tales* reads like a dream poem or a vision.

Yet she argues that over this 'superficial incoherence', over this dreamy quality, is an order of some kind. Again she suggests audiences of the time would recognise and accept this dream-like air, and that this, no less than the storytelling genre itself, must be examined as a tradition in order to see how, why, and where Chaucer departs from it. She argues that this quality at least partially enables Chaucer to interlace and juxtapose thematic patterns so that all his ideas, together with the forms of his writing, are 'explored and developed through superficially discontinuous narrative' (Cooper, 1983: 71). What Cooper does not say directly is why Chaucer would want to do this in the way that he does. Perhaps Chaucer's choice of this genre permits an open, fluctuating style where multiple views and perspectives can exist side by side with each other, the very contrariness of some of the tales and voices compounding the effect.

Cooper examines a range of approaches to the *Tales*, each of which offers an initial way in. One is to explore the poem thematically. Cooper identifies many themes each linking individual tales as well as groups of them. She refers to fortune, Providence, suffering (including the suffering of good women), brotherhood and friendship, 'female saints and wikked wyves', tidings or public opinion, tales, and voices. She traces motifs such as the love triangle or girl with two lovers (seen in the tales of the *Knight*, *Miller*, *Merchant* and *Franklin*), and demonstrates how the presentation of this idea cuts across genres, how imagery links the tales involved, and how they relate to each other, so a lengthy exploration of images describing Alison in the *Miller's Tale* is set against the depiction of Emily in the *Knight's*, for example.

Cooper also examines voice and layers of narrative. She notes that the tales are not told sequentially, and that layers of narrative build up. Her model for this is the *Nun's Priest's Tale* which she terms 'a kind of story-collection in miniature that works through receding layers of narrative'. She identifies an outer narrative which is its original teller, Chaucer, followed by the pilgrim persona who observes the contest and repeats the tale told by the fictional narrator, the Nun's Priest, who, in turn, tells of the cock, Chauntecleer. The narrative moves inwards. Chauntecleer also tells stories recounting his own dream as well as the dreams he has read of in his 'auctour'. One of these was told by another dreamer to his companion, and so on (Cooper, 1983: 5). In fact Cooper views the *Nun's Priest's Tale*, with its layers of narrative, its themes, and different styles as a model of the *Tales* generally; it is a crucial story, a 'Chinese box' (Cooper, 1983: 244). When you have read the rest of her argument you could return to this notion and test it out.

According to Cooper, another way of searching for the order of the *Tales* is via the dramatic frame of the pilgrimage. She suggests that this is more than a connecting device. Instead, it actively encourages each tale to lead out of another

> dramatically and thematically; and very often, the setting serves to alter the stories told. A tale that would mean one thing in isolation can be given a very different meaning running in parallel or on a collision course with the first, when it is put into the mouth of a particular teller or juxtaposed with certain other tales. The *Pardoner's Tale* is thus at once moral (inveighing against avarice) and flagrantly immoral (as serving to line the Pardoner's pockets) (Cooper, (1983: 5).

Do you think there is any value in this sort of approach? Is the *Miller's Tale* made more resonant by reading it in conjunction with the *Knight's*? Can the Pardoner's avarice and implicit criticism of the Church be set against the *Friar's* or the *Summoner's Tale*? Is there any connection between the *Wife's Prologue* and the *Nun's Priest's Tale*?

How is the latter tale to be read? In contrast to or parallel with which other tale?

Also important is the order of the fragments, the arrangement of themes, and the general progression of the pilgrimage. Cooper accepts too the existence of some initial semblance of order established by the issues raised in the *Knight's Tale* and the *General Prologue*. She clearly states, however, that taken on their own, these, and the areas mentioned earlier, remain inconclusive. She argues that instead there exists 'a kind of cobweb effect' (Cooper, 1983: 69). By this she means that each tale might be read sequentially or not, read alone or in conjunction with others, begun at the start or in the middle, for their connection is present but not rigidly structured or finally fixed.

Cooper believes that Chaucer's revisions, sketchy fragment order or initial groupings of tales, and changes made as tales are reassigned to speakers, all testify to his central and overriding concern for what a story-collection could do (Cooper, 1983: 69). His underlying idea was one of juxtaposition where 'each story defines its own possibilities' (Cooper, 1983: 63). Explorations of individual tales are therefore only of partial value for ultimately the stories belong to a whole. By juxtaposing different genres and assigning tales to certain speakers, Chaucer is able to open up perspective. Cooper describes it thus:

> The tales can suggest criticism of their own genre; adjacent tales qualify or parody particular elements in each other; the choice of a particular narrator can mean the abuse of story for personal insult, or personal gain, so that a tale is not allowed to express its own meaning but is slanted away by the circumstances of its telling from any inner 'truth' it might contain. (Cooper, 1983: 208)

There are many ways in which you could apply this comment to the stories we have chosen to focus upon, especially when you remind yourself of the sorts of things discussed in the earlier part of this study. Is the mix of rhetorical devices and numerous styles of the *Nun's Priest's Tale* simply for comic effect, or is there an underlying intention to highlight the limitations of a genre that relies upon such 'tricks of the trade'? Is the *Miller's Tale* a parody of courtly love made more resonant by its juxtaposition with the *Knight's Tale*, and exposing the limitations of both extremes, spiritual and elevated love, and the earthy and lewd? What, if anything, does the Pardoner gain from his frank admission of his trickery and ulterior motive, and how does this affect our reading of his chosen story, a moral sermon preaching against the very sins of which he himself is guilty? Is the *Wife's Prologue* her 'excuse' to bombard her audience with her own distinctive and contentious views? Is the fairy story she tells a manipulation of the genre to ensure that it expresses her own personal 'truth' about love and the relationship between the sexes? Are you able to use Cooper's comment as a starting point for discussion of further issues?

Cooper stresses multiplicity, suggesting that Chaucer intended to avoid 'doctrine' despite his appeals to it, to fracture the notion of authority and, instead, to raise rather than answer questions. His search is not for a fixed truth, and there can be no winner of the storytelling contest because the tales do not impart knowledge or compete to adopt stances; instead they remain open to a range of different perspectives. Reconsider the *Nun's Priest's Tale* in this light, especially as earlier Cooper identified it as a model for the *Tales* generally. Chauntecleer appeals to written authorities and dream-lore to insist upon his own very masculine authority and fixed definitions of literature and life, all of which is challenged both by Pertelote's practical folklore or wisdom and his own subsequent experience with the fox. At the end of the tale Chaucer, or his fictional speaker, asks what his tale means, attempting to insist upon it as a morality tale (VII 3437–46). Does Cooper's remark illuminate this story in any way?

Where Chaucer does give his tales a moral or a clear meaning this is always 'countered by contradictory elements within the tale, or by a contradictory moral in an adjacent tale' (Cooper, 1983: 241). Some tales even seem to have no deeper meaning at all (Cooper suggests the *Miller's*, *Friar's*, or the *Squire's*), though these are always highlighted by their juxtaposition to others that are full of them. Similarly others, like the *Merchant's Tale*, have a concluding morality that seems 'inadequate' when set against the narrative, and where the story itself points to 'so many other possibilities' (Cooper, 1983: 243). Cooper's final conclusion is that the tales must be read interrelationally for

> *The Canterbury Tales* demands to be looked at as a whole; anything less will yield only partial and restricted results. Its meaning finally cannot be separated from 'al that writen is'. (Cooper, 1983: 244)

As already suggested, Cooper's detailed analysis of individual texts is fairly rare. Her remarks on two tales deserve brief mention, however. Once again she returns to the *Nun's Priest's Tale* to draw attention to the means by which Chaucer uses this story to undercut all notions of authority or fixed truth. She notes the way in which the tale appears to validate the truth of dreams, for example, for Chauntecleer's own dream is a prophetic one. At the same time the tale indicates that it remains a work of fiction, set in the time when birds and animals could speak. Dreams, she argues, are special for Chaucer and remain linked to ideas about the nature of literature. They are fictional yet creative and imaginative, but also have the power to offer a higher truth than normal life might recognise. Dreams are, of course, central to the narrative of this tale, yet, as a whole its meaning remains elusive. Its narrative layers and different voices serve to compound the problem of its meaning and in this respect, Cooper believes it is a paradigm for the *Tales* itself. The Nun's Priest gives numerous hints about the 'sentence' of his story, none of which are definitive, while Chaucer-the-pilgrim only records that it promised to be 'myrie'; behind all this is the figure of the author himself (Cooper, 1983: 7).

Secondly, Cooper examines the *Miller's Tale* in relation to the *Knight's* which precedes it. She suggests that the *Miller's Tale* is a reduction of its predecessor in every aspect. Where the *Knight's Tale* is resolved by planetary influences, the *Miller's* deals in the commonplace and everyday. The rivalry of the lovers is crude rather than chivalrous. Alison is certainly not the impartial observer Emily is. In terms of poetry too the contrast is clear with the *Miller's Tale* going twice as fast as the *Knight's* in any oral reading of it, while

> the French and Latin elements of the vocabulary of the *Knight's Tale* are largely replaced by light German monosyllables, the weighty set speeches by colloquial exclamations and even the rhythms of folk verse.

At this point she quotes lines 3477–86 where John, terrified that Nicholas's learning has made him ill, shakes him awake (Cooper, 1983: 114).

The vocabulary is also lower in tone – 'wenche' and 'lemman' replacing 'lady' for instance. At the same time the *Miller's Tale* remains a story free of the expected moral tag normally associated with the fabliaux genre, and Cooper suggests that if it has any meaning at all it can only be found in relation to the *Knight's Tale*, in its alternative reading of a 'world of cheerfully amoral disorder, with no metaphysical depth whatsoever' (Cooper, 1983: 115). Interesting though this analysis is you might like to consider your own earlier exploration of this tale. Does Cooper's reading offer any different or additional insights? Had you already identified these points in an independent reading and, if so, does this in fact negate her view that the tales must be read together?

Summary

Cooper's suggestion that the *Tales* is a poem that is deliberately resistant to reading, a poem which opens up and multiplies perspective, is a valuable insight. So too are her notions concerning the structure of a work that is a story-collection, one that, in effect, tests the limits of writing. Her focus is upon writing and the writer, with Chaucer playing with conventions and subverting his time's expectations concerning authorial 'truth'.

Inevitably such an overview leads to generalisation. Her stress upon the intertextuality of the *Tales* tends to denigrate the possibility of studying individual works in isolation, something which might offer important insights. Is it fair to say that her approach also requires you to have a sound knowledge of all the *Tales* as well as the different genres and conventions it uses? Does she have a tendency to suppress individual voices in the poem or to ignore its historical context except in connection with the literary world? Does she focus upon Chaucer's writing at the expense of his ideas? Is it fair to say that sometimes she ends by saying little, so anxious is she to qualify or to emphasise the importance of juxtaposition? Her perspective is interesting, but at the same time as she advocates Chaucer's open approach she gives us her 'authoritative' view of his intent. Do you agree with this or is it simply an accusation that might be levelled against any critic?

ALFRED DAVID[11]

David's favoured terminology is apparent from the moment he begins structuring his book. He has chapter titles such as 'experience v. authority', 'the bourgeois misanthrope' or 'the bourgeois sentimentalist', and describes the *General Prologue* as 'Portrait of the Christian Community'. His chapters have a tendency to order or group tales according to what they might reveal about their interests; are they stories of 'innocence', 'experience', or 'morality', 'comedies', or tales of 'chivalry'? The tendency, too, is for them to follow the structure of the fragments or run alongside the dramatic frame as he considers the questions raised by the texts. More generally, he opens with discussion of Chaucer's other work, especially his use of narrators for, as his title indicates, he is a critic concerned with Chaucer as an author or an artist. David remains concerned with the development of Chaucer's poetic skills, with his 'art' and, as the subsequent discussion should reveal, with Chaucer's ability to balance his art and the 'morality' required by his audience. David's approach is schematic and searches for order, for a line of development that he assumes stops at or culminates in the *Tales*.

This humanist approach focuses on Chaucer's literary skill. David argues that Chaucer was subject to the pressures of two orthodoxies, social and moral, as well as his own inclinations as he set about learning his craft. Central to his argument is the belief that the poet found it both difficult and, ultimately, impossible to reconcile the two. The conflict is centred upon his era's notions of authority and his own artistic vision, something clearly reflected in the *Tales*. David describes Chaucer as a master of illusion ultimately sceptical about poetry's ability to express moral truths (David, 1976: 5–6).

Though Chaucer writes in the form of dream vision, or else is heavily influenced by it, for David there is a vein of naturalism that runs throughout the work and almost convinces us that his stories are 'real'.(You could consider the *General Prologue* in this light or the *Wife of Bath's Prologue.*) A medieval author was required to stress morality, to educate and instruct as well as entertain. Yet, says David, as a poet, Chaucer, like others before and after him, wished to

> make us aware of the superficial and illusory character of the life we perceive through the senses, which is no more than a reflection seen in a glass darkly, and to awaken our minds and our hearts to the spiritual reality beneath our sense impressions. (David, 1976: 6)

Do you find David's language overblown here? Does his style detract from what he is trying to say, which is that the inherent tension in all good medieval writing is that, in order to express its message or morality, it must provoke an awareness that our human everyday 'life' is transitory, an illusion? So powerfully realistic is Chaucer's depiction of that everyday life that he is in danger of detracting from the spiritual message he is required to convey, or as David puts it, 'the images of art take on a life of their own' (David, 1976: 6). Chaucer himself had doubts about this expressed in the '*Retraccions*' at the end of the *Tales.* For David, however,

> Chaucer's effort to reconcile the 'auctorite' of his age with the 'experience' of his inner vision is precisely what makes his poetry great. (David, 1976: 6)

David traces Chaucer's early works in an attempt to demonstrate the poet's awareness of what a writer should be, and the ways in which he developed and refined this to take it beyond the authorial constraints of his time. In particular he focuses upon the various uses of 'voice', beginning with the naive and humble dreamer-narrator, and moving to something more complex in the *Tales*. It allows Chaucer to multiply perspective and avoid fixing ideas or truths or, as David expresses it 'The *persona* thus becomes the poet's device for avoiding commitments and judgements' (David, 1976: 219). Consider the role of Chaucer-the-pilgrim or Harry Bailly in the dramatic frame in the light of this remark. The voice of the first-person narrator of the *Tales* is inconsistently employed. For David this is part of the illusion of the pilgrimage itself and, because it reappears when you least expect it to, also serves to break that illusion. For example, when Chaucer-the-pilgrim is called upon to tell his two tales, Chaucer reminds us all that *he* is the 'author of everything' (David, 1976: 220).

David sums up Chaucer's achievement in writing *The Canterbury Tales* in almost reverential terms:

> In writing *The Canterbury Tales* Chaucer came to master the art of illusion but at the same time to regard with growing skepticism its potential for expressing moral truths. The relationship between teller and tale often comments poignantly on the inadequacies of poetry, and each teller shows some new face of the poet's strumpet Muse. (David, 1976: 7)

Do you think David is correct to stress the relationship between tale and teller here? Does the *Pardoner's Tale* express the inadequacy of poetry or fail to offer some moral truth when it is set against what we know of the Pardoner and his profession? Similarly, is the Wife's story unable to fully or realistically satisfy her demands for a loving relationship, especially since its chosen form is a fairy-tale? On the other hand, how does the Nun's Priest's character or voice relate to the tale he tells? Does his story offer us some kind of proof of the inadequacy of literature?

Before examining in some detail the application of David's theories to the Wife of Bath, let us consider some of his comments on the *Pardoner's Tale* and its relation to its teller. At one stage he considers the moment when the Host attacks the Pardoner and the Knight is forced to intervene (IV (C) ll.919–68). He suggests that the Pardoner has tried to cut himself off from the company with his insulting invitation to offer to his relics, but that he is finally pardoned himself, first by the Knight who seeks to restore harmony, and secondly by the others, including Harry Bailly whose hand he shakes. The following is a lengthy quotation from David:

> Vice and blasphemy are, in the end, also impotent and have no power over the things they seek to harm. Evil is only the negation of good; sin, only the denial of love. Ultimately only good and love can come of them. The kiss of brotherhood between the Pardoner and the Host is a comic but meaningful reassertion of the brotherhood of man, which the sworn brotherhood of the three rioters has just marked. Just as the Pardoner has failed to isolate himself utterly from his fellow pilgrims, so no man can wilfully withdraw from the Christian communion. If the Pardoner can be pitied by the Knight, the *miles Christi,* then perhaps he may be forgiven by Christ himself. It is at least an open question. (David, 1976: 204)

Though tentatively expressed, David immediately characterises his approach to this, and other tales. He firmly links the story told by the Pardoner with its speaker in his suggestion that the evil pact between the rioters is the inverse of the bond uniting all the pilgrims. Where the rioters are wicked and beyond redemption, the pilgrims are good and united in Christ. The Pardoner's attempt to disassociate himself from this company ultimately fails, thus demonstrating the lesson that no one is beyond Christ's forgiveness. What this idea does is closely link the tale and its teller, but it also might be said to impose an order, a harmony, or a stress upon Christian 'morality' where maybe none exists. David's emphasis is also upon the dramatic framework of the *Tales* itself, a point you need to reconsider in relation to Cooper's comments about structure and order discussed earlier.

It is perhaps true, however, that the actual tale the Pardoner relates is often ignored in favour of an exploration of its fictional narrator. David, on the other hand, ties the two very closely. His discussion springs from a belief that the tale is a sermon about sin, but, more importantly, centres on death. The three rioters, drunk before noon, promise to live and die for each other, to kill Death itself, an oath blasphemously parodying the Trinity and making a travesty of Christ's death with its promise of redemption for all. Death is personified as an old man whom the three meet on leaving the tavern, an old man who begs for the release of death. He carries the burden of the world's sins and, interestingly, points the three in the direction of their own deaths, symbolic of the death of the soul as well as physical death.

David sees a link between this old man, Death, and the Pardoner. The Pardoner too wanders from town to town, and he too sends people up the 'croked wey'. Where the Pardoner is aggressive and frankly wicked, the old man is humble, meek, and courteous. Yet, says David,

> The old man does indeed tell us something about the Pardoner, but something more profound than what the Pardoner has already told us about himself: that he is an evil man. The old man tells us about the frustration, the suffering, and the self-destructiveness of evil. (David, 1976: 199)

Death may appear as an old or a young man, and the Pardoner tries to seem young. Does his portrait in the *General Prologue* bear this out, or his professed desire for wine and women? The three rioters are also young, and their vices those that the Pardoner boasts are his own – drunkenness, blasphemy, avarice. They are comrades just as the Pardoner and the Summoner are. They vow to slay Death, while the Pardoner promises to absolve men of their sins. But, David claims, the *Pardoner's Prologue* reveals his false forced bravado, seen in the way he reiterates 'I wol' and 'I wol not' (ll.444–51), like a hysterical child:

> The Pardoner is, in short, a young–old man, and the confrontation between the three rioters and the old man in the tale brings to the surface a moral and psychological conflict that has been latent all along. (David, 1976: 200)

The old man longs for death but cannot find anyone to swap youth for old age. It is this, says David, that shows the flip side of the Pardoner who wearily carries the burden of sin. His tale involves two sets of characters, each expressing one aspect of his own personality. The rioters, their swearing, their greed, and boastfulness, resemble the side displayed in his *Prologue*. The old man reveals what the Pardoner tries to conceal which is 'his despair of release, his isolation from human love, and his deeper alienation from divine love'. The Pardoner, quite simply, suffers for his sins (David, 1976: 201).

The rioters discover gold but find that it is Death. The *exemplum* of this tale contains an irony for it encourages its listeners to hand over their own 'death' or money to the Pardoner. The Pardoner tells the pilgrims that he is searching for gold. In reality, according to David, he is seeking Death. This is the Pardoner's sermon, one which is really about himself as well as a demonstration of his own manipulative cleverness. Yet the figure of the old man in his sermon 'also conveys the Pardoner's subconscious appeal for compassion' (David, 1976: 201).

David's view of this tale certainly achieves his aim of relating story to teller and offers an interesting psychological picture of this fascinating character. Is he right to stress the notion of Chaucer as a Christian moralist, which is what is implied here, or to thoroughly dissect this problematical speaker almost as though he was real, and not fictionalised?

David's analysis of the Wife is considered to be an influential one. He suggests that she comes alive off the page, while her own confrontation between experience and authority is a notion central to Chaucer's art. As a character she is saved by her laughter and sheer joy in life. In particular David draws attention to her recounting of her time with her last two husbands where her memories flood in to give us a strong sense of her personal experience as she looks back upon her life with nostalgia, speaking of 'my world', and 'my time' (David, 1976: 148) (III (D) ll.469–562, 586–627). Here David's stress is upon Chaucer's development as an author, seen in the *Wife's Prologue*. She makes her case against clerical and patristic authority by citing personal experience, her revelation of her personality and life enthralling the reader. Yet she also cites many authorities too. Her *Prologue* is thus a satire which cuts two ways:

> It is a satire of a woman preaching; at the same time it is a satire of preachers and their art.(David, 1976: 137)

The Wife participates in the act of 'glosynge' reserved for the male cleric, and her use of it turns it into a 'travesty'. David defends her against the charge that she is hypocritical, or even that a medieval audience would have laughed at her:

> The Wife of Bath's authorities may easily be turned against her, but her very citation of those authorities reveals a knowledge of life that challenges the theoretical moralist in a much more profound way. (David, 1976: 141)

David argues that her chosen topics confront the way people, and women in particular, were told to behave. In depicting herself as joyful and sexually generous, she challenges the notion of flesh as sinful. Later she confronts masculine supremacy by offering the female as superior. She paints herself as a 'shrew', but her advice to other women, about how to achieve the upper hand in marriage, reveals what is wrong with marriage at this time as well as informing us about medieval images of woman (David, 1976: 143). Would you agree with this or do you think that Chaucer is presenting her as a monster whom his audience would despise?

David argues that in marrying her men for money Alison demonstrates a sound grasp of the basis on which all marriages were contracted, but her desire is not for wealth. Rather, she wants that which economic dependence denies to women, namely power. With it too comes freedom, yet she continues to crave love, something she regards as 'like any other commodity to be bought and sold in the world's market place'. This stress upon economics is also seen in the way the Wife tells how she gains 'maistrie' in marriage (David, 1976: 144). David explores this in some detail, suggesting that her jealous husbands try to restrain her, prevent her from spending money and enjoying sex. Unable to realise the extent to which she is imbued with ideas about marriage, the Wife only knows that 'her body has a market value' where she can either 'sell' her 'bele chose' or keep it for her husbands (David, 1976: 146). She marries Jankyn for love, an emotion she has wanted all along, but she seems unable to comprehend this relationship except in the way she has always understood life – which is according to the laws of supply and demand. In support of this view David refers us to her comment that

> 'Greet prees at market maketh deere ware
> And to greet cheep is holde at litel prys.' (ll.522–3)

For David, Chaucer's intention is to satirize this figure, but at the same time he uses her to expose the shallowness and cynicism of a profoundly anti-feminist era (David, 1976: 146). Equally she is a character at once energetic and larger than life, but also tinged with sadness for she constructs a fantasy around herself. Denied love by the very nature of medieval marriage, she instead hungers for power, turning herself into the stereotypical shrew or virago,

> the monster of the antifeminist myth incarnate, but if she is a monster she is a Frankenstein monster. It is men who have made her so aggressively masculine. The humor as well as the pathos of her situation is that the masculine role she sees herself as playing is at odds with her feminine nature. (David, 1976: 146)

She becomes a typically domineering wife, and effectively plays out the role of the husband, because she has no other model on which to base herself, so imbued is she with the authoritative teachings of the medieval world. Thus she cries 'alas' that ever love was sin (ll.614–16) in her failure to understand why she is so wrong, simply assuming that her life has been determined by astrology (David, 1976: 153).

Once again this is a persuasive dissection of this complex figure and Chaucer's reasons for creating her. The dangers of such a perspective have been indicated earlier (see the section on Hansen); it is interesting to note that David, Hansen and Aers all arrive at similar conclusions about this speaker via very different routes. It is now up to you to form your own opinions.

Summary

David is in many respects a highly persuasive critic as well as a slippery one. His focus is upon the act of writing, on what is unique about Chaucer's poetry and his artistic development, especially the tension between morality or didactism, and creating a lively, naturalistic or lifelike work of art. Thus his concentration is on the manipulation of different voices and narratorial stances.

Several questions spring to mind. Is he in danger of being swept away by Chaucer's 'realistic' portraits of speakers like the Wife or the Pardoner, even though they are not the only voices in the *Tales*? How can he relate tale to teller in stories like the *Nun's Priest's Tale*? Does he overemphasise the importance of the dramatic frame or ignore social tensions perhaps informing Chaucer's art? Do you need a knowledge of Chaucer's work generally to make sense of his argument or does this not matter? Finally, his book title contains the word 'morals', as in Chaucer's poetry and the demands made upon it by his audience. Does it also imply that David has his own moralistic frame that he imposes as a semblance of order upon Chaucer's *The Canterbury Tales*, or is this an unfair criticism?

8

Further Reading

The previous chapter offered an exploration of the views of four major critics in the field of Chaucerian criticism and invited you to make up your own mind about the strength of their very different approaches. Discussion was mainly confined to the poems under consideration in this guide but, of course, each critic also deals with other poems written by Chaucer. Equally, their views are only some of many alternative approaches to the same, and other tales and you would do well to consider other critical works. The following is a small selection of either complementary or highly contrasting perspectives. Full titles appear in the Bibliography at the end of this section.

Like David Aers, Stephen Knight (1986) offers a politicised reading of the *Tales*, in his case a clear Marxist perspective, one which he shares with Sheila Delany (1983 and 1990) whose interpretation is, however, very different. She also writes from a feminist viewpoint as do Jill Mann (1991) and Carolyn Dinshaw (1989), whose work is particularly stimulating, in my opinion. Like Alfred David, E. Talbot Donaldson (1970) is a traditionalist and a humanist with some interesting points to make about the *General Prologue* and the voices of the dramatic frame. An entirely Christian and moralist approach, probably largely discredited but nonetheless interesting as an example of how a rigid perspective narrows reading, is D. W. Robertson (1962), while V. A. Kolve (1984) offers an extremely interesting interpretation of the stories in the *Tales* by exploring iconography combined with patterns of imagery. There are numerous critics writing about Chaucer and you may well care to look at others. If you do, it might be useful to bear in mind the questioning approach suggested at the start of the previous chapter.

Several critics have stressed the intertextuality of the *Tales* and its individual stories. Your own reading will undoubtedly range beyond the texts set for study and the following is a brief indication of the tales you might enjoy reading, or which might illuminate the ones you have already read.

The theme of learning, or knowledge versus ignorance, appears in the *Nun's Priest's Tale*, the *Miller's*, and the *Reeve's Tale*, while both its type of genre and its use of authorities may be seen in several other stories. It is a beast fable with a 'message' or *exemplum*. The tale of *Melibee* is didactic and quotes extensively from authority. The *Manciple's Tale* is another beast fable. The *Wife's Prologue* cites authorities as does the *Friar's Tale* and the opening to the *Merchant's Tale*. The Summoner preaches too, giving us a satire on sound and wind, upon language itself. If your interest is in forms of writing, then look at the *Monk's Tale* with its collection of tragic tales, the Parson's serious sermon, the romances of the Squire and *Sir Thopas,* the Pardoner's morality tale, the Wife's fairy story, or the Second Nun's saint's life. Similarly, there is a collection of fabliaux like the *Miller's Tale*, which includes the tales of the Reeve, the Shipman, the Summoner and the Cook.

The *Miller's Tale* might be read as a contrast to or an inversion of the *Knight's*, while its presentation of women demands comparison with Emily in the *Knight's Tale,* Custance in the *Man of Law's*, Griselda in the *Clerk's*, Dorigen in the *Franklin's*, May in the *Merchant's*, perhaps Virginia in the *Physician's Tale,* and, of course, the Wife herself. Other tales also deal with marriage and sexuality; read the *Shipman's*, the *Reeve's*, the *Wife of Bath's Tale* and *Prologue*, and the *Merchant's Tale*. Chaucer also engages with the anti-feminist tradition in the *Wife of Bath's Tale* and *Prologue*, the tales of the Parson, the Nun's Priest and the Merchant, while money and sex are linked not just in the *Wife's Prologue* but in the *Shipman's Tale* too.

Religion is an important aspect of the *Pardoner's Prologue* and *Tale*. You may also care to read the *Friar's*, the *Summoner's*, the *Monk's*, and the *Prioress's Tale*, and set these against the ideal of the

Parson's Tale. The notion of 'gentillesse' features in the *Wife's Tale* and in the *Franklin's*. Again you may care to read the ordered notion of chivalry *apparently* presented by the *Knight's Tale*.

Finally, the *Tales* contains several strong, and hence often problematic, speakers, and in this respect it might be interesting to compare the voices of the Wife, the Pardoner and the Canon Yeoman.

What about Chaucer's work in general? A strong element of the *Tales* is the interplay between various characters, plus the roles of Harry Bailly and Chaucer-the-pilgrim. If your interest is in narration and voice, it might be useful to examine the narrators of *Troilus and Criseyde* and *The Legend of Good Women*, possibly setting these against an earlier example such as *The Parliament of Fowls*. Similarly, if your interest is in the presentation of women these first two might again merit exploration. Dreams feature strongly in the *Nun's Priest's Tale* as well as in the *Book of the Duchess*, *The Parliament of Fowls*, and the *House of Fame*. Finally, the themes of writing or Chaucer's employment of authority set against experience, so clearly witnessed with the *Wife of Bath's Prologue* and in the *Nun's Priest's Tale*, also feature in *Troilus and Criseyde* with its focus on the contrast between ideal and more practical ways of behaviour. In addition, the art of writing is a central concern of the *House of Fame* and *The Legend of Good Women*.

Notes

6 The Context of Chaucer's Works

1 Women found it especially difficult to gain acceptance both in their own right or as authoritative writers. Margery of Kempe, an ordinary illiterate woman, used three separate scribes to transmit her fascinating life story, *The Book of Margery Kempe*, which told of her struggle as a married woman with thirteen children to establish herself as holy in the face of much hostility from masculine authority in particular. Other women, recognised as saints, achieved fame only because their lifestyles were admired by prominent and influential teachers and clerics. I am thinking here of someone like Mary of Oignies whose story was transmitted by James of Vitry.

2 Note the assumption that it is only women who might be guilty of this offence.

3 See the *Wife of Bath's Prologue* and the *Merchant's Tale* where Chaucer explores and sometimes subverts such views. You might then like to compare these portraits to that of Alison in the *Miller's Tale*.

4 It is interesting to note that the Wife of Bath's wealth comes, in fact, from her deceased husbands even though she is considered an expert in her trade.

5 Again, Margery of Kempe is a good example of this, struggling to gain her husband's agreement that it was no longer necessary for her to pay the 'dette'. They eventually made a pact that she could have her way so long as she continued to eat with him at all times, thereby avoiding his public shame.

7 Critical Approaches to Chaucer's Work

[6] Material is taken from the following: Aers, David (1986) *Chaucer* (Brighton, Harvester Press Ltd) and Aers, David (1980) *Chaucer, Langland, and the Creative Imagination* (London, Routledge and Kegan Paul). In the first of these he examines the *Book of the Duchess*, the presentation of Criseyde in *Troilus and Criseyde*, and the following in the *Tales*: the *Nun's Priest's*, *Summoner's*, *Pardoner's*, *Second Nun's*, *Prioress's*, *Melibee's*, *Miller's*, the *Wife's*, *Merchant's*, *Franklin's*, ideas of lordship in the *Knight's* and the *Clerk's*, money and commercial interest in the *Shipman's*. In the second, his focus is upon Criseyde again, and the *Summoner's*, *Parson's*, *Franklin's*, *Merchant's*, *Clerk's*, *Wife's*, *Knight's* tales as well as the *Wife's Prologue* and the *Pardoner's*. In each case he adds to rather than repeats ideas.

[7] Both of these examples are taken from *Chaucer, Langland, and the Creative Imagination.*

[8] See Elaine Tuttle Hansen (1992) *Chaucer and the Fictions of Gender* (Berkeley; Oxford, University of California Press). Her analysis cuts right across Chaucer's works to include the *Book of the Duchess*, the *Parliament of Fowls*, the *House of Fame*, *Troilus and Criseyde*, *The Legend of Good Women*, and, in the *Tales*, the *Miller's*, the *Clerk's, Merchant's*, *Franklin's*, the *Wife of Bath*.

[9] Medieval notions of the body were extremely slippery, and gender not as fixed as we might think. The body was regarded as a continuum with masculine and feminine characteristics at either end rather than as two distinct entities. A hermaphrodite, someone of no fixed gender, might then simply be required to 'opt' for one or the other and stick to it without any problem or disapproval.

[10] Material is taken from Cooper, Helen (1983) *The Structure of 'The Canterbury Tales'* (London, Duckworth). In it she makes at least passing reference to all of the tales offering an overview rather than a detailed analysis.

[11] References are from David, Alfred (1976) *The Strumpet Muse: Art and Morals in Chaucer's Poetry* (Bloomington and London, Indiana University Press). He examines a range of poems including all of Chaucer's earlier ones before moving on to the *Tales* where he

looks at the *General Prologue*, the *Miller's*, the *Nun's Priest's*, the Pardoner and the Wife in particular. Essentially you will find something on all of Chaucer's works and all of the tales.

Bibliography

Aers, David (1980) *Chaucer, Langland, and the Creative Imagination* (London, Routledge and Kegan Paul)

— (1986) *Chaucer* (Brighton, Harvester Press Ltd)

Cooper, Helen (1983) *The Structure of 'The Canterbury Tales'* (London, Duckworth)

David, Alfred (1976) *The Strumpet Muse: Art and Morals in Chaucer's Poetry* (Bloomington and London, Indiana University Press)

Delany, Sheila (1983) *Writing Woman: Women Writers and Women in Literature, Medieval to Modern* (New York, Schoken Books)

— (1990) *Medieval Literary Politics: Shapes of Ideology* (Manchester and New York, Manchester University Press)

Dinshaw, Carolyn (1989) *Chaucer's Sexual Poetics* (Madison; London, University of Wisconsin Press)

Donaldson, E. Talbot (1970) *Speaking of Chaucer* (London, Athlone Press)

Hansen, Elaine Tuttle (1992) *Chaucer and the Fictions of Gender* (Berkeley; Oxford, University of California Press)

Knight, Stephen (1986) *Chaucer* (Oxford, Basil Blackwell)

Kolve, V. A. (1984) *Chaucer and the Imagery of Narrative* (London, Edward Arnold)

Mann, Jill (1973) *Chaucer and the Medieval Estates Satire* (Cambridge, Cambridge University Press)

— (1991) *Geoffrey Chaucer* (London, Harvester Wheatsheaf)

Robertson, D.W. (1962) *A Preface to Chaucer* (Princeton, Princeton University Press)

Index